FIVE MEN

WHO BROKE

MY HEART

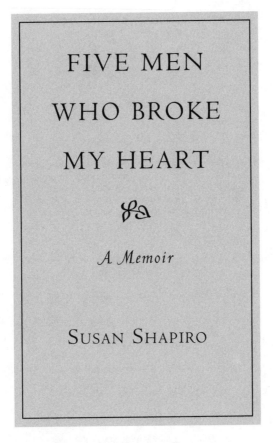

FIVE MEN

WHO BROKE

MY HEART

A Memoir

SUSAN SHAPIRO

DELACORTE PRESS

FIVE MEN WHO BROKE MY HEART: A MEMOIR
A Delacorte Book / January 2004

Published by Bantam Dell
A Division of Random House, Inc.
New York, New York

Book design by Virginia Norey

Delacorte Press is a registered trademark of
Random House, Inc., and the colophon is a trademark
of Random House, Inc.

LIBRARY OF CONGRESS CATALOGING IN PUBLICATION DATA
Shapiro, Susan.
Five men who broke my heart: a memoir/Susan Shapiro.
p. cm.
ISBN 0-385-33723-X
1. Shapiro, Susan. 2. Women—United States—Biography.
3. Man-woman relationships—United States. I. Title

CT275.S4392 A3 2004   2003053239

974.7/1043/092 B 21

Manufactured in the United States of America
Published simultaneously in Canada

BVG   10   9   8   7   6   5   4   3   2   1

for CR, forever

Author's Note

Names, dates, and identifying characteristics of many people portrayed in this book have been obscured for literary cohesion, to protect privacy, and so my husband won't divorce me.

FIVE MEN

WHO BROKE

MY HEART

1

I slipped on the black slingbacks I'd borrowed from my best friend, Claire. The last time I risked such high heels was at my wedding. I tried to walk without wobbling, praying that the added height hid the nine pounds I'd gained since he last saw me. In two decades as a journalist I'd never been this nervous for an interview. Yet I'd never interviewed anyone I'd been in love with before.

I hadn't seen Brad in ten years. In ten minutes he was coming back to see me. Not to say "I'm sorry," "I can't forget you," or better yet, "No woman has ever been able to replace you." No, after a decade, Brad was finally seeking me out again—to help him get book publicity.

I pulled a tight black T-shirt over my long flowing Indian skirt, adding silver bracelets. Too Greenwich Village, which I feared I was, but sexy, which I feared I wasn't. At least I had a tan. Whipping the shirt off, I switched from my sports bra to a black Wonderbra, turning my respectable breasts into major knockers, a Gloria Steinem acolyte suddenly Living Barbie. I would rather be dead than dowdy for this reunion. I tried a tighter black tee—much better—spraying Opium perfume down my faux cleavage. Lining my lips Midnight Red, I caught a spark from my diamond ring in the mirror. My hand was shaking.

Out of the thousands of days we'd been out of touch, Brad could not have picked a worse one to reconnect. Six months before my fortieth birthday, I was staggering through a vulnerable stretch of midlife crises: my "no-book-no-baby summer." That morning I'd received two faxes. The first, from my gynecologist, summed up results of fertility tests explaining why, for the last year, my husband, Aaron, and I had been unable to conceive a child. My reproductive system seemed to be in fine working order. Aaron's wasn't. The problem was his low sperm count and the lack of his sperm's "motility." According to the doctor, the medication he'd been taking wasn't increasing the amount of his sperm or making it swim any faster.

The second letter, from my agent, listed the last five publishing houses that had "passed" on the novel I'd spent five years writing. It felt like she was saying, "The only baby you have is ugly, we don't want it."

I threw both letters down the incinerator in the hall, destroying the evidence before anybody else could see it. Rushing back to answer the phone, I thought it would be Aaron, calling from the airport to say his flight was delayed. But it was Brad, the man whose children I could have had twenty years ago, now a Harvard professor, saying, "Hi Sue. I just landed in New York. I have a book coming out," as if we'd last spoken yesterday. Brad's timing always sucked. Today it was so bad it seemed destined.

"Hey, that's great," I'd said, equally casual, feeling surprisingly jazzed to be on the phone with him. I had an urge to see him in person. "What are you doing for lunch?"

"Coming to see you," he'd answered, presumptuous as always, though I had just issued the invitation.

"Bring me a galley. If I have time, maybe I'll write about your book," I threw out, turning my big date with Brad into a business opportunity to avoid anxiety. Or was it rage?

What the hell did he mean—he had a book coming out. *I* was the writer! I'd recited Robert Louis Stevenson's "I Had a Little Shadow" by heart when I was two. My mother taped it, I had proof. In first grade I won an award for filling out the most notebooks in the history of Shaarey Zedek Hebrew School, twelve hundred blue notebooks crammed with Hebrew letters I couldn't read. In my family, achievement was redemption.

According to Shapiro legend, my father proposed to my mother by saying: "I just got into medical school in the Midwest. You coming or not?" They fled the Lower East Side and eventually settled in suburban Michigan. Of their four offspring, I was the first and the only girl. I was quickly followed by Brian and Eric, both redheaded and freckled like my mother, and Michael, the youngest, whose hair was dark as mine. I always thought the defining event of my emotional landscape was being usurped of firstborn power thrice, by three brilliant science-brain brothers. Picture it: Queen Sheba for seventeen months, then dethroned, dethroned, dethroned.

While I had my mother's twenty-twenty vision, my brothers were all nearsighted like my father. They wore gold-rimmed glasses with thick lenses and viewed the world as their laboratory. They dissected frogs in the kitchen sink—merrily holding up body parts that pulsated after they were amputated—and kept calves' esophagi in the freezer and live bees in jars in the refrigerator. (The first to freeze won. Then they'd try to resuscitate them.) By the time I was ten, family dinners were dominated by "The Disease Game," where one called out symptoms, the other diagnosed.

"Forty-two-year-old Cambodian refugee vomiting blood?" asked my father.

"Schistosomiasis!" jumped in Brian, my oldest, biggest, loudest brother.

"Good! You know more than your old man already." My father spooned gravy on his steak. "Thirty-four-year-old white woman with perforated uterus."

"Could be endometriosis," guessed the middle son, Eric, the diplomat.

"Botched abortion, probably," weighed in Michael, the smallest Shapiro. "Pass the potatoes."

I'd eat alone in my pink room, memorizing Sylvia Plath's *Ariel* and plotting escape.

I thought I'd found it at sixteen, when I started the University of Michigan in Ann Arbor. Yet on my first day of freedom, freshman year, I gravitated right to Brad, a patronizing, macho biology major.

"Do you have a light?" I stopped to ask him in the dormitory lobby.

He took the Virginia Slim Menthol from my lips and broke it in two.

"Who the hell do you think you are?" I yelled. I'd already decided to be a raging feminist poet. I had no use for this intrusive, oversized prep in a blue-and-gold sweatsuit.

"I'm Brad," he said. "Don't smoke, it's bad for you."

I noticed his gigantic shoulders. Out of all the first-years, his were the broadest. "So are you," I said, digging into my backpack for my own match. I found one, lit another Virginia Slim Menthol, and walked away, smoke trailing.

He followed me to my dorm room, where he scanned my schedule (Romantic Poetry, Journalism 101, Modern Drama, Psych. of Deviant Behavior) and declared it worthless. An alliance with a male, fraught with fierce rivalry—what could be more familiar? I declared him worthless and he wrestled me to the floor. I put him in a choke hold my brothers had taught me, never imagining the hold he'd wind up having on me. Or that it would last, off and on, for fifteen years, from age sixteen to thirty-one. The worst years to be off and on in love with anybody.

By the time I was twenty, I'd graduated, sworn off Brad and the Midwest and braved New York City solo. I earned my masters degree in English and toiled, for thirteen thousand dollars a year, as a peon at *The New Yorker*, eventually finding a way to almost make a living freelancing and teaching. Six months after school ended, Brad surprised me by moving to Manhattan too. Not for me, but for an opportunity to work as co-CEO of a medical research company. When that failed, he decided to get his Ph.D. in biology. Why did he get to publish a book? I didn't invade his space by curing cancer.

Half linebacker, half bespectacled science nerd (like the males I knew best), Brad hadn't taken an English class since tenth grade. His letters to me, in his sloppy third-grade handwriting, were hidden in a shoebox in the back of my bedroom closet where my husband wouldn't find them. The most profound one read, "If I was capable of loving someone it would be you, but I'm not so I don't."

During our brief phone conversation, he'd said he was a tenured professor (I was an adjunct) and that he'd wound up selling that "failed" science company for seven figures. He also mentioned (okay, I asked) that he was dating—but not married, engaged, or living with—Kim, a twenty-four-year-old graduate student he could have twenty children with. To make Satan's Circle complete, my returning WASP-alpha-male-ex had published a self-help book on primal instincts and self-destructive impulses, like the kind I should have suppressed when I told him to pick me up at my apartment.

It could have been worse. I could have been single and idiotically hoping I would end up with Brad, as I had for eleven years after college. What had thrown me was the way he slept with his knees over my legs, locking me in. I liked to sleep as far away as possible, back turned. But the minute he lost consciousness, Brad's heavy limbs draped over me like an avalanche. I couldn't move, more physically entangled than I'd ever slept with anyone. Sure that it meant something other than that's how he slept with women. Plural. Always plural.

Not that it mattered now. I was happily married to Aaron, who didn't sleep as close but stayed. Aaron was ten years older, four inches taller, twenty times wittier, and a thousand times more loyal than Brad. I was thinking in numbers, subtotalling everything: years, mistakes. Not that I was comparing. This was just a lunch interview and I'd done hundreds. Expertly, on deadline. Hell, I'd taught an NYU class called "Interviewing" and didn't even need textbooks. When the doorman buzzed, I raced to the intercom, tripped on Claire's slingbacks, and fell to the floor, wrenching my ankle. I knew I couldn't handle grown-up shoes, but it was too late to change. I brushed myself off and limped to the door.

Brad walked in and said, "Hi."

"Hi," I answered.

We hugged quickly, then I took a long look at him. He didn't look so hot. He was in khaki pants, a blue blazer, and white shirt buttoned to his neck, stiff. The only time he'd dressed hip was the year I took him to The GAP. I picked out three pairs of tight black jeans and black T-shirts, helping him try them on until a salesgirl yelled, "Only one in a dressing room!" and threatened to call the manager. His brown hair was too short, a crew cut he'd settled on after graduation. I liked him better with the dark, curly, white boy's Afro I used to run my fingers through. He'd gained weight too. Not fat, but too big. With short hair his features seemed splattered across his face like a platypus—huge ears, nose, brows. Oh no, I still loved him.

To keep my hands busy and my heart from bursting, I handed him things: an anthology that had reprinted two of my essays, my most impressive clips from *The New York Times* and the *Washington Post*.

"I found most of these on-line," he said. "I did a search."

"You did?" I gave him my two previous books—a poetry collection called *Internal Medicine* and a humor book, *The Male-To-Female Dictionary*.

"I've already read your humor book," he said. "It was hysterical."

"You have it?"

"Amazon.com," he said.

The hidden perk of publishing: it left a trail that could be easily followed if someone from the past wanted to find you. Or was that the hidden peril?

He handed me his galley. I opened it and began reading his intro about how the male hanging fly used food to attract fertile females, in a manner similar to the way a Wall Street trader wined and dined a young model, quickly winning her over. It was entertaining, for sociobiology, though comparing modern human mating rituals to animals' was a way to rationalize sexism. This was about books, right? That's what I'd e-mailed Aaron about the meeting. I'd written that my old college friend Brad Wentworth was dropping off his book, which I might write about. I changed "friend" to "boyfriend," then took the "boy" out again.

"Armed with a little knowledge, we can control our primitive urges," I read aloud from Brad's book, quoting him back to himself, basking in the irony.

"I know. The blind leading the blind," he said, smiling. I'd forgotten how self-deprecating he could be; it knocked the edge off his arrogance. He took his galley from my hands and put it on the coffee table. It was gray and puny, but next week his book would be out in hardcover. He put my books down next to his. Mine were paperbacks. Smaller. Inadequate. Not imposing enough. That was the problem lately—everything led back to what was missing.

I thought baby lust had used up my envy energy, since every other female in the world appeared able to have children. My mother the redheaded domestic goddess, a cross between Rita Hayworth and Lucille Ball, married my father at nineteen and produced four kids in six years.

Once when I was freaking out about gaining a few pounds, my shrink, Dr. G., asked, "Why do you like your body best when it looks like a thirteen-year-old boy's?"

"I don't know where my weight obsession comes from." I'd shrugged. "My mother was always thin."

"Except when she was pregnant," Dr. G. said. "So she'd get fat and a terrible thing happened—a new brother. And another. Then a third. No wonder . . ."

My sister-in-law Monica, once my sophisticated *New Yorker* colleague, snagged my brother Brian, now a trauma surgeon. She moved to the Michigan 'burbs, where she traumatized me all over again by popping out three perfect babies in the last four years, becoming the daughter my mother always wanted.

My brother Eric's wife, Jill, a scientist, went back to work weeks after delivering a gorgeous baby girl—to add to the proud grandparents' photo montages. I became preoccupied with my nephews and nieces, begging to hear them gurgle over the phone, spending money I didn't have on adorable mini black leather jackets and stone-washed jeans from Baby Gap. My apartment was filled with pictures of other people's children.

Swarms of female friends—even my single, gay, and/or New York ones—had already figured out a way to get inseminated. I actually found myself jealous of the ones who miscarried. I couldn't even manage a miscarriage! Then everyone else I ever met came to my doorstep with their published books, which pissed me off way more than the babies did.

Three former students had books out. A fellow NYU teacher (with two sons) called for daily advice about her traumas with her book's agent, editor, and publisher. My *New York Times Book Review* editor assigned me Al Roker's infertility memoir. Even the fucking weatherman got a hardcover! (And two daughters.) Publishing PR people put me on their lists for review copies, bombarding me with packages reminding me of what I couldn't accomplish myself. When I called my forever depressed and single pal Dana and said, "What's up?" she sang, "I'm engaged and I sold six books this year!" Six!

"Dana does kids' and joke books. They're not books, they're ooks," Aaron said, using our code for commercial drek, giving me a foot massage. I was lucky to be married to this kind, nurturing man who critiqued my work, line edited, and proofread. Wasn't I?

It was the first time I'd questioned my choice of spouse in five years of marriage. Isadora Wing, the witty heroine of *Fear of Flying*, warned that "five years was the crucial point in a union—when the sheets you got as wedding presents were wearing thin." Ours had just ripped. "It was time to decide whether to buy new sheets, live with each other's lunacy forever and have a baby, or give up and go back to playing musical beds." Getting my spiritual guidance from the fictional femme fatale out for a zipless fuck, I decided to have a baby. I convinced Aaron (who was ambivalent), went off the pill, read the books, ordered baby guards for the windows, and saw the doctor. I started dreaming of our babies, naming them. There was Jacob, who was tall, with Aaron's glasses and brown curly hair, and Lilly, a smart little girl with my grandmother Sophie's Slavic eyes. Not being able to have a real baby skewed the light, as if Aaron and I were all of a sudden flawed as a couple. We didn't work together biologically. Our family history couldn't progress. Something was internally amiss.

This visit by my longest-lasting former potential mate—with his book on breeding behavior—was an omen. If I'd married Brad, I'd have children by now, but we'd surely be divorced. If I was single, I could have his baby without marriage. Married to someone else, I could actually still bear his child, I couldn't stop myself from thinking. Indeed, it was the fifteenth day of my monthly cycle. There was a slight chance I wasn't finished ovulating. I pictured jumping Brad on the living room floor, getting pregnant, and moving to Boston. But I couldn't stand Boston. Maybe I'd get knocked up but tell Aaron it was his child. I'd thrown away my birth control pills two months before I told Aaron I was off them. I was willing to trick my husband into having his own baby. Couldn't I just trick him into having someone else's?

I stared at Brad. He looked more uncomfortable than I felt, if that was possible. He reached into his briefcase and handed me more things: A page from his publisher's catalogue showing that his was the lead book on their fall list. A starred review in *Publishers Weekly*. "I found six typos in the galley," he said. "I changed 'Bradley' in my bio to 'Brad.' It seemed more confident, to the point. What do you think?"

I thought he still loved me but was hiding behind clips. Mr. Studrocket had morphed into a neurotic fellow freelance writer obsessed with seeing his name in print. Biology Alien turns into my soul mate. Five years too late. Was it too late? Damn, I still hated him.

Miraculously, twenty thousand dollars' worth of therapy kicked in and I heard Dr. G.'s voice minimizing his hardcover, highlighting the relevant fact: He lived alone. The diagnosis was conclusive. Love or no love, Brad couldn't do it! It wasn't me! I was the closest he'd ever been to anyone, he'd often confessed. At forty-two, he had chosen a student almost half my age, as if twenty years later he could still only handle half of me.

He looked around, taking in my woodsy, elegant living room. The black moiré couches, laced with lime and purple satin pillows, were surrounded by antique book tables and torch lamps. What a nice nest I'd finally managed in this chaotic city. Part urban chic, part flower child artsy. I was seeing it through Brad's eyes. It was comfortable, yet sleek enough to be intimidating; he was sucking it all in.

He read the caption of the framed original *New Yorker* cartoon of two martians flying over Washington Square Park, where nobody notices them. One turns to the other and says, "I don't know, they loved us in Michigan."

"That's perfect." He laughed. I'd forgotten what a full, throaty laugh he had. "I bet you knew the cartoonist. Remember when I visited you at *The New Yorker*?"

That was my curse, I remembered everything.

He ran his hands over the oak bookshelves, catching my honeymoon picture in the silver Tiffany frame. "You've moved up in the world," he said.

He had known me in my three-hundred-square-foot, dusty, book-strewn studio on Horatio Street. The last time we'd made love was in that little Greenwich Village hovel, on my gray frameless futon on the floor. Brad had crawled out at 6 A.M., getting dressed. "I love you," he'd leaned down to whisper. I was stunned he'd used the word. Even more stunned with his next sentence: "I'm moving to Boston tomorrow." He wasn't asking me to join him. He let himself out. I couldn't speak or get up.

Now I plopped down on the black leather chaise so I wouldn't trip on the high heels again. He sat across from me on the couch. "So, Dr. Freud," he said. "What do you think?" His old nickname for me—he thought I overanalyzed everything—used to turn me on.

"Why do you ask?" I wondered if he'd get it.

"It all started with my childhood," he said. "Ready to go to lunch?"

Lunch meant I had to move. It was amazing I could still breathe. I checked out the window overlooking Broadway. It was raining. Oh no. I could barely walk in these heels in my apartment, let alone on wet sidewalks. I glanced at Claire's alluring sandals gracing my size nine canal boats, then at Brad. I thought of Robert

Lowell's line, "I'm tired, everyone's tired of my turmoil." The charade was over.

"It's raining." I stood up. "I'm gonna put on sneakers."

"No, keep them," he said, catching my eye.

Keep the illusion, he was begging. I want to remember you tall and thin and sexy and sixteen.

"There's a cheap Chinese/Japanese place around the corner." I figured it was my farthest teeterable distance.

As we left my apartment building, Tony—Aaron's favorite doorman—was eyeing us. I sauntered slowly down the street, pretending I was statuesque and graceful, holding a black umbrella. Brad walked next to me, not too close, getting wet. At the restaurant we took a table by the window. He number-dropped the fifty-thousand print run and eighty-thousand-dollar ad budget for his book, then said, "You're wearing green. No more all black?"

I noticed the moss flowers on my skirt. I'd unconsciously chosen my one outfit that wasn't all black, to send him a subliminal message. In the years without you I've added color to my life. I'm flowery, fun, fertile.

"Nice blurb from E. O. Wilson," I said, feeling nervous, overly ripe, about to explode. "I never saw *Publishers Weekly* star a self-help book. Impressive. I thought of a few editors I can pitch a profile to."

"It's nice to see you again," he said.

"You're really calling after all these years to get help with book publicity?" I blurted, as hurt as on the day he left. "Are you insane?"

He shook his head vehemently at the accusation. "No. We don't have to talk about my book. On the phone you said bring a copy, which is the only reason . . ."

"Is this like when I called you to say I was getting married?" His time was up. I wanted to know what he wanted, if not book publicity. Lost friendship? Approval? One last mind fuck—or real fuck—

for old-times' sake? Yet I was the one who had suggested lunch. More troubling was what I wanted from him.

I replayed our final phone call, five summers ago, when I told him about my engagement. He'd asked about Aaron, then concluded, "Well, he's ten years older. When he dies, you and I will get married in our old age." Was it sick? Hostile? Sweet? He could only use the M-word from the safest distance possible.

"I'm teaching a class in Ann Arbor next term," he said. "Made me think of you."

I flashed to our young naked bodies wrestling on the floor of his Arch Street dive, his muscular legs over mine, pinning me down all night, as if only in sleep he was scared I'd escape his grip and get away. I opened my notebook, pulled a black Flair pen from my purse, and started asking too many questions.

2

Two days later, I received an e-mail from Brad@Harvard.edu under the heading "Stormy Weather." I opened it to find six words: "hard to see you. raining since." I was taken aback. I was the wounded party here and I had almost recovered. I had sublimated my confusion and longing into writing an article about Brad, completing a thousand-word rough draft. Turning Brad's life into a pithy profile would finish something off. I could control this version.

Two years earlier, I'd interviewed another guy I'd dated, one who collected meteorites. First *The New Yorker* paid me twelve hundred dollars to run it as a "Talk of the Town" story. When they killed it, *The New York Times* picked it up for two hundred dollars and ran it in their Sunday City section. It made a good clip, though Meteorite Man wound up hating the piece and has never spoken to me again. Aaron suggested I do the same with all my exes.

It was 2 A.M. Aaron was gone for the week. I liked it when he went away. I stayed up later, threw things out, walked around with fewer clothes on. I was wearing the little black silk nightgown he'd bought me for our last anniversary, which, he'd complained, I never wore for him anymore. Sitting at his desk I scanned his tall, overstuffed shelves. He was a junk collector who saved everything:

newspaper articles he never read, stacks of take-out menus, all the little Post-it notes I'd written to him, even "Thanks for doing the laundry. Love you." We'd had a fight when I'd thrown out ninety-nine of the hundred white yarmulkes from our wedding he'd stashed in his closet. "It's romantic!" he'd yelled. "One is romantic!" I screamed back. "A hundred is psychotic!"

When we married, we agreed to file our books together, by subject. Aaron segregated "Baseball," "Basketball," and "Football," finding "Sports" not specific enough. He needed individual headings for "Civil War," "WWI," and, "WWII," aghast at my suggestion that we dump them all in "History." When he deemed "Comics" its own category and demanded separate space for "Humor" and "Comedy," we decided his boy books would live in his den, aka The Bat Cave. Problem was, he hoarded fiction and memoirs too, leaving stacks everywhere—the window ledge, table, floor, bathroom. "You can't read eight books at the same time," I complained. That was the problem with marriage: nothing stayed neat or where you expected it. When he wasn't around, I stuck the books back in their rightful place in the living room.

I wasn't just rescuing authors Aaron had absconded with. I had justification for infiltrating the reclusive Batman's lair. It housed our only computer. I preferred using a typewriter, my black IBM Selectric Correcting III, which sat in the middle of my desk. I hated computers, didn't have one, didn't want one. Then NYU, where I taught evening journalism classes, insisted I be available to my students by e-mail. Aaron offered to share his laptop. In screaming matches three nights in a row, he taught me to use it. I had never imagined having a joint AOL account could pose a problem.

Yet I felt guilty seeing Brad's message on my husband's Power-Book, let alone reading it over and over, a spy about to crack a dangerous code: "hard to see you. raining since." It was hot in Aaron's office. I didn't open the window or turn on the air-conditioning. The back of my thighs stuck to his desk chair as I leaned over his laptop, continuing my long overdue tryst with his once biggest threat.

"Why stormy?" I e-mailed Brad. "Guilt? Regret?" The one benefit of middle age was being too tired for bullshit. "You seem so on top of the world." Cliché, erase. "You seem great. Rich, Ivy League professor with a new book and new twenty-four-year-old." So what if I sounded petty? I was. I sent the message and went to the kitchen for a diet soda, returning *Portnoy's Complaint* to fiction, in case I needed it. When I came back the upbeat male AOL voice said, "You've got mail." Brad@Harvard.edu was awake. It freaked me out a little, like he was in the next room.

"You said when I left for Harvard I'd get one more gold star on my forehead, but still be empty inside. You were right," Brad answered.

Wow! When had I said that? Good line. All these years later he remembered my insult. I was flattered. But after the hardest, saddest, babyless months of my life, humbled. "I probably said that because I wanted you to stay in New York," I told him. "You had just incinerated my heart."

In the living room was the hand-painted box Aaron had bought me on our honeymoon in Jamaica. I kept my weed in it. I'd been off the stuff (along with cigarettes and alcohol) for almost a year, while we were trying to get pregnant. But if I was going to be barren and unpublished, I figured I might as well be stoned. There was one last thick joint left for just such a revelation. Putting on Dylan's *Blood on the Tracks*, enhancing my whole nostalgia trip, I took out my thick red photo album. I found my favorite Polaroid of me and Brad, taken the first week of college. I was thin, cute, and sixteen, the youngest in my class, two years early and proud of it. I was wearing Levi's and a tight burgundy leotard that showed off my figure, which Brad was staring at. I was looking into the camera. When we met, I was involved with another man, which, in retrospect, clarified everything.

I took deep puffs, replaying the first party freshman year. It was crowded, smoky, and smelled like beer. Brad took my hand and we danced to Gloria Gaynor's "I Will Survive." For a nerd, he could dance. He was fast, limber, and playful, pointing his finger and singing, "Go! Walk out that door!" As a slow tune came on, the lights dimmed. He wrapped his oversized arms around me like he owned me, his hands rubbing my neck. When the long sweaty song was over, we retreated to the Angela Davis lounge. After refusing to have sex and warning him about David, my rugged Canadian swain whom I was sure I'd wind up marrying, we made out on the couch till 4 A.M. Flustered by my leotard, Brad's hands couldn't find the way to my skin.

"You've got mail" startled me. I stubbed out the joint, rushed back to Aaron's office, and clicked so many times the computer squawked. Finally it stopped and six more words came on. "You weren't the only one hurt." Playing victim—now I really detested him. Before I could respond, he was back again. "I've only been seeing Kim for six weeks. I already want to escape." I knew she was a recent acquisition! He'd been rejecting me for twenty-four years, her whole life.

"Why was it stormy seeing me?" I demanded, high and dizzy. "Because I looked so old and seemed so angry?"

"You look exactly the same," he said.

"Nice avoidance," I quipped. "Don't tell me you're getting nice."

I remembered the first time I had finally consented to making love. Senior year, drunk on rum and diet Cokes, I barged into Brad's dingy bedroom on Arch Street at three in the morning, wearing my tightest jeans, black high-heeled sandals (kind of like Claire's, come to think of it), and braless blue halter. "I want you," I'd told him.

"You snap your fingers and expect me to jump?" he said, grabbing me and throwing me to the floor. He untied my top and pulled off my jeans and panties in seconds. I was a princess used to sweet talk and gentle caresses. He was a mean lover; I was a goner.

He tied my wrists together with the halter string, pinned down my legs, squeezed my breasts too hard. The viciousness was mutual. A frustrated tomboy, I bit his neck, then wrangled my arms free and scratched his back with my long nails, leaving scars like I meant to.

"Can't you fuck me harder?" I taunted.

"Shut up, bitch," he yelled. "I didn't give you permission to speak."

"I don't need anyone's permission to speak, Tarzan," I laughed, climbing on top of him.

"You've got mail" rang again. "I still love your brain," he said.

He still loved my brain. Man, did he know me well. The ultimate compliment, what a genius. He was in again.

"I've been reading your poetry book. It's amazing," he wrote, as if he could possibly endear himself further. "Especially 'Double Vision.' I loved that poem."

Love—he used the word twice, concerning my brain and the poem yet. I was shocked that he'd picked that poem, which was inspired by my dream that he'd had a car accident. I had published it in *Poetry East* five years before, when I was still in my Sylvia Plath/ Louise Gluck stage. It was about a married woman in her marital bed, dreaming of an old lover who was in a full body cast. She screamed out in her sleep. The last line was: "He's not dead yet, the husband said."

"You're the 'he,' " I told Brad. "But pretend I never told you that."

"Okay," he answered. "As if I could ever forget."

My heart was pounding. I was out of breath. I touched his words on the screen. As if I could ever forget.

"You still didn't say why you wanted to see me," I typed. No response. I recalled Dr. G.'s interpretation, that the dream meant I was admitting to myself Brad was too damaged.

I checked my other e-mail, biding time. I read two editors' notes, four letters from colleagues asking for advice. People always came to me with their problems. I wondered whether it was because

I seemed so strong or so nuts they figured I'd be empathetic. There was one from "HOTCHICK66," a blue-haired, nose-ringed girl from my NYU feature writing class: "I told my shrink that you were in therapy too." When a student asked how I'd made it as a freelance writer, I answered, "Ten years in therapy," and had subsequently been getting many "I see a shrink too" e-mails. I was playing the role of good hippie mother, since I couldn't be a real one.

There was an e-mail from Aaron: "Met with three producer piranhas in a row. Sick to my stomach. Will phone tomorrow. Me," he wrote, making Brad's attention to my psyche and poetry seem even sexier. I wasn't sure if it was Brad's love, body, or sperm I wanted. I'd settle for feeling the way I used to feel at sixteen, when everything was still possible.

As usual in times of need, I turned to my best friend, Claire, whom I'd known since I was born. Her mother and my mother were best friends and fellow baby machines. They each produced quartets: dark-haired girl to complement a trio of boys. Sundays, our fathers and brothers played touch football on the lawn. Our hopelessly glamorous mothers were cheerleaders and lemonade servers.

"Susie, will you bring out more ice?" my mother yelled.

"And the cookies, Claire," her mother added.

"We're the maids," Claire whispered.

Flunking the role of "Mommy's Little Helpers," we sneaked to the man-made lake down the block. There we chain-smoked cigarettes, painting our toenails blue on the edge of the broken picnic table. Unable to compete with our Supermoms, Claire and I eventually chose the one arena they hadn't conquered and became Serious Career Women, feeling perverse satisfaction in referring to them as housewives.

Then, after all the kids went away to college, our mothers began thriving businesses. My mother became a party planner, Claire's mom started a local magazine, mastering the whole female timeline, showing us up again. Although everyone kept telling us what lucky girls we were, this was the scenario we felt born into: we couldn't win. No wonder Claire was my pretend sister and mirror—five foot seven like me, with size nine feet, big shoulders, and an uncannily similar sadness.

I punched the name Claire Lyons in my computer address book, then sent: "Emergency! Brad's back." Now an architect with international clients, she was designing a Gucci store in Madrid. Was she checking her e-mail? I knew there was a way to check to see if she was checking, but I couldn't remember what it was.

"My introspection isn't that interesting," Brad responded at last. "Even when I hated you, I knew we'd stay friends. I was in New York, decided to call."

"Where were you when my books came out?" I asked him. "Or when I got married? I didn't want you to see me such a mess." After I sent that message I went to answer Aaron's note. But "You've got mail" rang again. I felt especially paranoid, as if Aaron could hear from L.A.

"You've done so much, I'm in awe," Brad's next missive started. "I think you have my disease: the more I accomplish the more worthless I feel . . . as if achievement were redemption."

Hey! I'd said that first! Many times! It was my line. (I could prove it because I'd stolen it myself from a poet I used to know.) Brad had memorized every stupid thing I'd ever told him. Did he do that to all his "friends"?

"I don't feel accomplished. I feel like a has-been who never quite was," I told him. "I wake up lost, homesick in my own room. Like I've been wrong about everything."

I recollected our four-hour conversation at the end of senior year, sitting in the dorm's parking lot in my ugly orange Cutlass. I'd wanted a black Camaro or a silver Trans Am, but they would have taken six weeks to order. The orange Cutlass was the only one on the lot I could drive away, so I did. Brad and I were supposed to meet friends at Dooley's Pub to celebrate his being made

Phi Beta Kappa. He was in his angst-ridden philosopher stage, rambling on about Sisyphus pushing the rock up the mountain. "Falls down every time," he said.

"Then why is it worth it?" I'd asked, pulling out a cigarette. "Love?"

"Doesn't exist," he'd said, breaking it in two.

"Not in the least," I'd agreed, resting my head on his shoulder. A wanna-be slut, my only problem with casual sex was that afterward, I always fell in love. Not normal "crunches," as Claire and I called them, or having the hots. The loitering, twisted, eternal kind.

There was another e-mail from Brad, but I was too tired, crashing. My cute little trip down memory lane had become an endless tunnel. I'd had enough, but for once he wanted more than I did.

"We all have ways of deceiving ourselves. The important thing is to believe in one's own importance," he said, adding "André Gide."

Quoting someone else. What was the matter? I wasn't good enough?

High or not, I was aware enough to know I'd crossed a line. It was worse than sexual. I even knew why it was happening. Like Brad, I was feeling empty inside. There was nothing as easy as reheating an old instrument of self-destruction. I typed my finale for the evening: "Never tickle a sleeping dragon. J. K. Rowling."

I closed the computer, turned off the lights, stuck Jimmy Breslin's *I Want to Thank My Brain for Remembering Me* and Mary Karr's *The Liar's Club* back in "Memoirs," where they belonged. Creeping into the bedroom, I shut the window and slid into my side of the king-size bed. Missing Aaron's body beside me, I was still finishing some old argument with Brad in my head. I closed my eyes, thinking how funny it was that I'd always slept better alone.

3

I was determined not to be rejected in selling a profile of the man who had rejected me. So I e-mailed my piece on Brad's book everywhere and took the first offer: the *Daily News*. When it came out Friday, I ran to get a copy. But the editor had not only butchered my original, he ran the article in the health section under the humiliatingly bad headline, "Primal Instinct Pow Wow." Instead of an author's photo, there was a half-page picture of an obese woman on line at a grocery store. In my haze of horror and embarrassment, I felt like the fat lady with no willpower in the picture was me.

"It's great. I love the fat lady!" Brad e-mailed me. He was using "love" again. For a guy who denied he'd even said it to me once in fifteen years, he was sure throwing the word around now. Though he wasn't even aware of it, all the inadvertent "loves" made me feel better. A few minutes later he added, "It's my favorite piece on the book 'cause it was written by you."

That good I didn't need to feel. Damn Brad, he knew how to push my buttons. He'd programmed my buttons. I went to the bedroom to straighten up. Aaron was due home at midnight. I made my side of the bed. I'd unintentionally left Aaron's side untouched. I fluffed up pillows and dusted the lamps and dresser, as if to sweep away the weekend's dirty thoughts.

I put my legs up on the living room couch and reread my article. It felt nice to be writing about Brad in something other than a secret sex poem. This was the public, sanitized version, now that we were grown-ups with official "ists," journalist and biologist, better than the former masochist and sadist.

In Aaron's office, I flicked on the laptop. Brad@Harvard.edu was waiting for me. "Paul called me from his cell phone, on the way to a meeting. He loved the article!" That word again. Not that it had anything to do with me. Brad loved it that his old roommate Paul saw his name in print. The last time I'd bumped into Paul he'd said that Brad had bought a black Porsche.

"Wasn't Brad the original antimaterialist?" I'd asked.

"Only when he didn't have money." Paul had smiled. "It's his new, sleek, black penis."

"How are you?" Brad continued. "What's with your book and baby? Any progress?"

Yeah, I gave birth to both yesterday, I didn't say. "Work's going well. I've sold eight pieces in a row. *New York Times Book Review, L.A. Times, Washington Post.*"

"Now who's avoiding?" he asked.

"As if you ever explained what you meant by 'stormy weather,' " I shot back.

"*Washington Post*—very impressive," he said. We were in our Pinter mode.

I pulled down the red photo album again, we had unfinished business. I turned to my thirtieth birthday loft party, the best party I ever had B.A. (Before Aaron). It was before Brad had moved to Boston. I found him, wearing the black jeans and shirt we'd bought together at The GAP. The clothes I'd chosen—a nice metaphor. Yet he was standing next to a tall dark-haired woman who must have come with a friend. Also in black, she resembled me but was less edgy, with a long Laura Ashley–looking pink scarf tied around her neck. He had his arm around her.

Details I didn't ask for flooded back. I was at my low weight, 123, in a tiny black flapper dress, fringe barely covering my thighs. I'd worn heels and sleek black Givenchy hose that made me feel held in and tingly. Brad arrived at the party at ten, kissed me hello on the lips, and said I looked "hot." The timing couldn't have been better. I was single, lonely, flipping out about turning thirty. He had brains and integrity, not to mention those incredible shoulders. He'd admitted he wanted a lot of kids one day. He would make a good father, I'd thought, getting us some champagne. But he disappeared into the black-clad crowd. He didn't come back to ask me for a dance, not even to our song, "I Will Survive." He'd been too busy picking up my pastel twin.

I'd never noticed this picture before, as if my camera had caught the scene so that, when I was ready, it would be waiting for me. Even in my sexiest dress, covering my thinnest body on my biggest night, Brad wasn't mine.

I marched back to Aaron's laptop, went on-line. "You left my thirtieth birthday loft party with that pink-scarf girl. I wanted to leave with you. Why didn't you stay?" I e-mailed, immediately regretting it. I had given too much away, I wanted my message back. Aaron had once said you could recall e-mail when both sides were on AOL, but Brad and I were on different systems.

Like the mating dance of the fireflies in his book, which flashed belly lights as a sexual code, we had our own signals. Brad's testosterone went into overdrive when I was taken. When I was available, he wasn't so interested. A one-creep-at-a-time girl with no patience, I'd find another guy to obsess over. Jealous, Brad would rush over, spin my silver bracelets around, and ask, "Why do you look so beautiful?"

"Because I'm with someone else," I'd say, offering to be his pal. But I wouldn't touch him, fueling his passion. Which he saved for one of my big breakup nights.

For years, when a relationship ended, I feared I'd never meet anybody else I'd ever be attracted to. Following the advice of another self-help book I'd read, on optimism, I "disputed myself," that is, proved my fear was unfounded. By calling Brad. (Self-help books always screwed me up.)

Brad would jump back into my bed, as if he was a doctor on call for such emergencies. Claire said he was like an inflatable Bozo: I knocked him down, he would pop up again. Or a modern tooth fairy who appeared with a prize every time my heart fell out. As he'd walk in, I'd play the Joni Mitchell song about the woman seducing a man while being "strung out on some other man." Brad liked me better strung out on someone else, amid the drama. He'd enter the hero, the returning lover saving me from the terrible fate of being alone with my pain for more than ten minutes.

What a fool I was, stuck in a night almost ten years ago, in a frilly half-dress that would no longer zip.

"I'm sorry," he said. "It was ninety-five percent my fault. I couldn't be close with someone then, still can't. It was me."

This was new. He was apologizing, accepting blame. It was an enticing offer, but I didn't want to be let off the hook. I'd analyzed my part of the Brad puzzle to death—how I'd made him into a bad boy, an impossible cad, an emotionally distant workaholic, like my father. Dr. G. said everything about Brad was "charged with past erotic energy." It wasn't really about him. I was turned on by male unavailability. If he'd ever looked me in the eye and said, "Let's get married and have babies," I would have bolted. When we got too close, I did bolt. That's what all the other guys were about. I couldn't do it either then; that's why I was with him. "I'm sorry too," I typed.

I recalled how fascinated Dr. G. was when, after years of talk about Brad's and my animal magnetism, I'd slipped in that I'd never actually come during intercourse with him.

"How can you say the sex was good if you never climaxed during it?" she'd asked.

"I didn't think it mattered *when* you came," I'd answered.

It had clicked with Aaron the first time we made love. He'd asked me to show him what I liked best, and tell him when I was coming, so I was honest and did. Brad never asked. So I used to come quietly during foreplay. Afraid that I'd finished too soon, I'd then pretend to have an orgasm the moment he did. He never knew I'd faked the timing. I thought of e-mailing him that bizarre little factoid, but decided "It's my favorite piece on the book 'cause it was written by you" was the exit line going down in this chapter of our shared saga.

Before I could turn off the computer, I heard sprightly music. An instant message from Claire. "Not Brad Brad? Stay away! I'll e-mail you a ticket to Spain . . . You're my only healthy, married role model, don't sleep with him. I couldn't handle it."

"Don't worry," I wrote back. "Trauma averted."

I laughed, realizing what I'd been doing—using lies and self-mythology to fill in the holes in my life. Aaron couldn't get me pregnant, so in my daydreams he died (never divorce, only death) and Brad returned to impregnate me.

The doorman buzzed to say I had a package. In the lobby were seven copies of Brad's hardcover. His male radar must have detected I was leaving him again. He signed the top one, "Our first Shapiro-Wentworth collaboration." Our first. What was next? E-mmaculate conception?

I carried Brad's books upstairs, wondering what to do with seven copies. In college, Dr. Rabkin, my favorite professor of a class called "Fantasy," analyzed Snow White and the Seven Dwarfs:

"They might have been little but there were seven of them." I stuck them on the bottom shelf of the bookcase, in the "Women's Issues" section, so the chance of Aaron seeing them was zero. Aaron had been gone a lot lately. I was relieved he was coming home. Writing a screenplay and television show the same season, he'd been cranky and preoccupied. He was obsessed with his work while I'd been immersed in mine: tracking my monthly cycle. I'd counted till day thirteen each month and peed into a cup to see if I'd be ovulating within the next twenty-four hours. If I was, I needed Aaron that night and the following morning. I warned him in advance. He obliged, happy to get on top of me for fast sex with a higher purpose. Then I waited fourteen days. For the first time ever, hoping I wouldn't bleed.

While he was away, I felt lost in a sexual fever. I kept pretending I was on top and Brad was brutal—taking me away from my life—which had nothing to do with Brad anymore. I came better remembering sex with him than having it.

I reread my entire electronic tête-à-tête with Brad several times, from start to finish, carried away for hours. It made me feel lighter and liberated. I wondered if disarming the past was a way to make peace with the present—or to avoid it. I thought of changing back into the black silk nightgown, but I'd thrown it in the hamper. I was wearing my usual T-shirt and sweats when Aaron walked in at 2 A.M. He looked tired, his long great hair lopsided from trying to sleep on the plane; he never could sleep on planes. He put down his suitcase and kissed me. "After we landed, the damn plane kept circling the runway," he said. "It took them ninety minutes to find a gate."

"I'm sorry. I hate that. How did your meetings go?"

"Same idiot bloodsuckers," he mumbled. He hated L.A. After ranting about why and how much he hated L.A. for the seven thousandth time, he asked how I was doing. I showed him three clips I'd accumulated that week, the one about Brad's book on top. He stood there, reading it. "Your piece is good," he said. "But his book sounds dumb."

Competitive or dismissive? I wanted to tell him what had happened with Brad, but he was too busy, trashing the idiot producers while unpacking and looking through the stack of mail I'd left on the coffee table.

"I heard from my agent. Bad news," I slipped in. "Week from hell."

"I'm sorry." He gave me a quick hug.

"Did you eat on the plane? Want something?" I asked, deciding it wasn't the time to tell him about the other fax. "Or is it too late?"

"If I can't get you pregnant, are you leaving me for someone who can?" he asked, sifting through invitations we'd say no to, catalogues we didn't order from, bills we had to pay.

"No. Of course not. Don't be ridiculous." It was my turn to put my arms around him. I always underestimated male powers of perception, blind to my own transparency. "I won't see Brad again," I said. "Not seeing him for so long made it intense. Ten years. The perspective." I took the mail from Aaron and held his hand, which drooped in mine. There was no spark between us these days, just quick sex twice in twenty-four hours, disappointment two weeks later. We knew each other too well. "Tell me about the night you met me," I said. "What did you think?"

"You were beautiful," he said, playing along despite the hour. "In your studio on Horatio Street, stacks of books all over."

"Did you think I was tall?"

"Very tall." He smiled. He was the tallest guy I'd ever fallen for; standing next to him made me feel petite. I pulled him down on the couch and sat close. He rubbed my back. "Tall, sexy, and strong," he said. Good, this was working. His hand kneaded the back of my neck. I'd missed him.

"And funny?" I put my hand on his leg.

"Very funny," he said. "Hard jokes, I was impressed." He had a theory that most women did soft jokes, though I forgot the difference. "And I remember your bathroom was filthy," he added.

"Screw you!" I socked his arm. "Can't you stay romantic for three minutes?"

"You asked," Aaron said. "I remember thinking, This chick is hot and does hard jokes but needs a maid."

"Brad's e-mail said 'I still love your brain.' Why don't you ever say that? It was the first compliment in years that made me feel good."

"He still loves to fuck with your brain." Aaron stood up, taking his bag into the Bat Cave.

I followed, moving the scripts on his faded gray couch so there was room to sit down. I knew he was out of it, but we'd barely spoken in a week. He expected to find me waiting in the exact same place, as if he'd left a bookmark.

"You never call me smart," I said.

"I compliment you all the time." He was annoyed. "I just called you beautiful."

He didn't get it, I always had to explain. "I grew up the only girl with three brothers everyone called brilliant. I was cute or pretty or adorable. That doesn't do it for me. Don't you know me at all?" I pleaded. "Why do I need ten thousand books and clips everywhere? To overcompensate. To convince everyone I'm smart 'cause nobody ever said it . . . to convince myself," I said. "I become what's missing."

"Now that's smart," Aaron said, patting my forehead. "You ugly pig."

4

August 2000
Rehashing Hamlet

I was invited to lecture at a journalism conference one Wednesday afternoon at a college way the hell out in Brooklyn. Two subways and a cab ride away. After committing to the date, I realized I'd been there once before. Nine years ago I'd made the trek to see my then boyfriend George, a theater professor. We were involved for a year and a half. He was my first lover after Brad left, and the last heart slayer before I met Aaron. Whatever happened to George? I wondered if he still taught there.

He was one of the leading heartbreak contenders of my life. This had to be fate. I immediately called the college and asked for George Silver, and he picked up on the first ring. I said hello, expecting shock. "How's it going? Aren't you giving a lecture here Wednesday?" he asked, no big deal, like I called him all the time.

"How did you know?" I asked.

"They put up fliers," he said. "I saw your wedding announcement in *The New York Times*."

Good, that's why Manhattan women splashed their good fortune in the Sunday paper, so their old cads could see it. "Yeah, five years ago," I said. "What about you?"

He said he was married too, with a son, still living near the college.

"Come by and say hi Wednesday," I told him. "My lecture will be in room 423."

Hanging up, I noticed that my palms were sweating. What in God's name was I doing? I had just remet Brad; I was still bouncing off the walls from that. Two weeks later George was falling into my lap. It felt like a scroll was unraveling my carnal chronology in front of me.

From ages thirteen to thirty-five, before I'd wed Aaron, I'd plunged, heart-first, five times. Once every 4.4 years. I was a serial monogamist love junkie, a romantic extremist with no sense of irony. After the recent rejections—of manuscript and motherhood—this summer, old rejection was easier. Remeeting a series of men who had unceremoniously dumped me was a weird remedy for a bruised ego. Yet it was cheaper than going back into therapy and I felt alive again, something kicking inside.

This was clearly connected to my upcoming big birthday and fifth year of marriage. God was telling me it was time to come to terms with my ill-spent youth. Or was I torturing myself by revisiting the potent sperm that got away? More likely I was bored, and masturbating with my past was more fun than working.

When a relationship ended, it always took me a long time to leave emotionally. Luckily the men left physically, often moving away within days of our severing. I imagined I elicited such great guilt or passion or intensity they had to flee. I tried to convince myself that I was winning. No matter how much I got hurt, the Village was mine and nobody, least of all a sputtering flame, could take it away. Still, after each breakup, I couldn't help but feel abandoned. Until I found a new boyfriend—who eventually abandoned me too. Until I met Aaron the workaholic, who managed to marry and abandon me simultaneously. Sometimes I thought the problem was that I'd flunked all five breakups. What if I'd done it wrong and had never really gotten over any of them?

After George left, I told Dr. G. my theory that old boyfriends should just die. "Breakups are worse than death," she said. When a mate passed away, you were left with good memories and sympathy. When a lover dumped you, you were expected to get over it in a month. Then, for the rest of your days, you were faced with the threat of seeing him happier with someone else.

That threat was upon me. I was a little jealous of the woman who shared a bed with George every night. I was a lot jealous that they had a child. The fear that I'd never have a baby was escalating, crawling into everything. In the bizarre logic of my infertility fog, George's baby was a stunning blow.

That night I told Aaron about my upcoming lecture, the coincidence that George worked there, his wife, child. "Wonder if he lost his hair," I said.

"If he doesn't show up, he's bald," Aaron offered, exhibiting no interest in my lecture or previous lovers, fleeing into the Bat Cave.

I never told Aaron the reason I waited two months to sleep with him when we met. It was because I was still with George. Not in reality, but a heart overlap.

Since calling George, I'd been sleepless, nervous that this event might not be the right place for an update, showdown, or attempt at neoresolution. I would have preferred reading from my best-seller at Barnes & Noble, weighing 123, my husband and four perfect children waiting in the wings, when a fat, bald, and homeless George happened in. Yet my cover was flawless. I was being paid to pontificate in my field, giving off the illusion of expertise. The college had even agreed to a car service. (I couldn't be witty and charming trekking two hours on two trains at 11:30 A.M.)

Furthermore, I was happily married to a very successful guy, had what resembled a good career myself, and was off of nicotine. I was nothing like the chain-smoking mess George had last seen crying hysterically on the corner of Horatio Street and Eighth Avenue, after he said he was sleeping with Diana, a wanna-be actress in one of his school plays. Nine years later I remembered her name.

I had fallen for George when he was geographically desirable, subletting a one bedroom on Jane Street, two blocks from me. We slept together (with just feet touching) on my gray futon, which I'd lodged on the wooden bed frame he gave me from his *Hamlet* set. I urged him to do theater, rather than just teach it, hooking him up with people I knew at The Kitchen and La Mama. All that came of my connections was his best compliment: "If I had met you in high school, I would have been a director."

I attributed our different levels of ambition to our fathers. Close in age, they both grew up in poor New York Jewish families. My father spent half of his childhood lugging window shades and blinds up and down the broken steps of his father's store on Delancey Street. When my Grandfather Harry refused to cough up my father's NYU tuition, my Grandmother Yetta stuck her head out the window and screamed, "If you don't pay for Jackie's college, I jump."

Though he wound up paying, my grandfather never forgave my father for forsaking the window shade business. Yet leaving was my father's medicine. Out of all the medical schools he was accepted to, he intentionally chose the one farthest from his family. He became a doctor, living the American dream, giving his kids the delusion that they could be anything.

George's father was a husky sports star in high school. Then he escaped to the exciting merchant marines. But when he married and started a family, he landed back in Brooklyn and took a job he didn't love. He was competitive with his son, berating him for being skinny and too sensitive. I decided that was why George was two people: meek Jewish Brooklyn boy and rambling heathen.

In public, George was timid, as if his father had scared the fire out of him. In bed, he was a caveman, fierce and aggressive, as if his masculine power could only come out in the dark. If each old boyfriend could be summarized by one body part, George's long penis was central to the story. It was the lure he used to entice me, the weapon he drew to betray me. We ended, after all, when he stuck it in someone else.

But this went deeper than the body. I was dying to know the catch, what my brain had omitted. With Brad, it was climaxing during sex. It wasn't orgasms this round. I always had them when George and I did it, leading me to believe that size did matter. (Until he split and I convinced myself it didn't.) Though he never liked how I reached nirvana. He was angry when I admitted I got off picturing him ravishing a female stranger.

"Then you're not really with me," he accused. "It's like you're not here."

From then on I kept my eyes open—but only literally. It turned out my fantasy was prophetic: I came best pretending he was doing what he wound up doing.

On Wednesday, to meet Heartbreak Number Two, I wore a knee-length black skirt. What was with all the skirts? I'd been stuck in jeans for decades. I was finally ready to look like a girl now that my girlhood was gone. I paired it with a loud turquoise shirt— all bright, happy, and counterphobically healthy. I didn't consider my Wonderbra or Claire's do-me slingbacks, which I planned to keep forever but wasn't silly enough to wear to Brooklyn. I chose wedged heels, more George anyway; he was pure granola. He liked his women natural: no makeup, no jewelry.

I was glad the black sedan from the car service was late. I was actually afraid to see George and for him to see me—older, heavier, made up, wearing the diamond ring and watch that Aaron had bought me. But the one time I wasn't in a hurry, there was no traffic. We made it over the Brooklyn Bridge in seven minutes. The driver dropped me off at the front gate of the college. I walked in the main building, which looked big and rundown and urban, with tons of students on their way to lunch or class. I stopped a pretty girl in T-shirt and ripped overalls and asked her the way to room 423. She looked twenty, my age when I'd started at NYU. She had a nose stud and three silver rings coming out of her lips. She pointed down the hall, to a set of blue-painted elevators. I felt old and sweaty. When did I become the teacher, wearing a watch and wedding ring and long sleeves? Didn't it hurt when she kissed?

I'd seen worse than the friendly audience in urban tweed gathered in the conference room. The chairman of the department seemed quite happy to meet me, shaking my hand and introducing me to several students and professors. From the side of my eye, I caught George walking in. He had hair, not at all gray, though it was cut shorter. Otherwise he was about the same: tall, lean, thick glasses hiding his brown eyes, a Jewish Clark Kent.

When we'd been involved I became thinner, tanner, more athletic, turning into him, wearing his uniform: faded jeans and crisp white shirts. People stopped us on the street to say what a beautiful couple we made. Not a compelling reason to pledge your life to somebody, Dr. G. insisted. Yet for a basically cerebral girl usually locked in her mind, it was dazzling, I'd countered.

When I first met him at one of my crowded late-night soirees, I almost missed him. Claire pointed him out and asked who he was with. I encouraged her to go flirt with him, but she said he wasn't her type.

"Your type is self-destructive and not the least bit interested in you," I told her.

"The blind leading the blind," she recited, our lifelong mantra.

I didn't notice George again until he was leaving.

"It was nice meeting you," I said at the door.

"You're the perfect little host, but don't waste your party chatter on me," he uttered, pegging me as a superficial socialite. Boy, was he off base. Didn't he know I'd marched, rallied, volunteered, had published in *The Nation*! I found his challenge mean-spirited and compelling. The next day I called him for a cup of coffee. We met at the Village Den, right between our apartments.

"Tell me, Susan, what was the point of that party?"

"I met you, didn't I?" I flirted, sipping my large diet soda.

"Did you say one thing the whole night you really meant?" He had coffee.

"No. Not a word. I have a fear of intimacy," I said. "Like you do."

"That's what you think?" He looked amused as he suavely lifted a Newport from his pocket to his lips. He lit it slowly.

"That's my diagnosis." I reached in his pack and stole one.

"If I get close, I turn into a pumpkin?" he asked, lighting mine.

"Or your father cuts your dick off," I said, being my usual pop Freudian self, not yet understanding why he looked at me as if I'd just cut off his.

It would have been over were it not for the fire truck pulling up Eighth Avenue. Smoke poured out the window of the dry cleaners and a crowd gathered. George forcefully placed his arm around my shoulder, took control, and led me to safety like my own personal fireman, an urban Robinson Crusoe. I rarely played damsel in distress and it turned me on, made me feel protected. He swept me out of the chaos on the street and into the chaos of his dark, messy apartment . . .

As I heard myself introduced, I switched to automatic pilot, walking to the dais and picking up the microphone. I cruised through amusing sound bites ("Journalism is literature in a hurry") and self-deprecating anecdotes (the time I interviewed Václav Havel on the dangers of European nationalism when I didn't know what European nationalism was). I offered uplifting adages ("Two pages can change your life") and divulged ten secret tricks of a freelancer ("Call a publication's advertising department, say you want to buy an ad, and they'll send you a list of upcoming special issues. That tells you what subjects their editors will be interested in for the next year"). Then I took questions.

"You mentioned that you're not supposed to send out multiple submissions," said a young guy in the back. "Why can't I just e-mail a piece to a bunch of editors and see who responds?"

"That's like asking someone out for a Friday night date. And before they answer, asking someone else out for Friday night. And then asking a third person," I said. "What if they all call and say yes?"

"When you started, how did you handle the rejections?" another guy asked.

"Ten years of therapy," I said, my standard answer, which always got a laugh.

I focused on the front row, ignoring George's presence, trying not to listen for his laugh. After the clapping and more handshakes, everyone mingled at a lunch spread of cold cuts, bagels, and pepperoni pizza. I nibbled carrots, noticing that George had stayed. We were all finished by two o'clock; the driver was to return at three. I had an hour to kill. I hadn't come all this way to wimp out now. I steadied myself for my second heartbreak interview.

"Time for a cup of coffee?" I asked.

"You don't drink coffee," he said, looking at his watch. "How about a tour of campus?"

"Great." Didn't he remember I'd been here once before?

"You were funny as always." He led me down in the elevator, through the lobby, outside. He liked it better outside. "Do you give a lot of lectures?"

"No. I'm researching an article. It's called 'Five Men Who Broke My Heart.' " I made up that title on the spot. Not bad. Yet blatantly admitting he'd broken my heart made me more vulnerable than I'd meant to be. I added, "There's four more, all across the country," warming to the title. It was catchy, slick, full of female bravado. George didn't have to know that every morning for a year after he left, I opened my eyes, saw he wasn't there, and started crying. A visceral reaction, before my mind was awake.

Shifting to reporter mode, I peppered him with questions, making Lois Lane work for me. I learned that his wife was Melissa, a teacher my age, not the Diana Slut of my old diaries. He first knew Melissa in high school, then remet her by chance three years ago, when he moved into the apartment she was subletting. I absorbed his answers and the charming how-we-met-story-for-the-grandkids with ease, especially since they wed two years ago. I'd beaten him to the altar. Yet his son, Max, who was ten months old, trumped me. George took a picture from his wallet.

"Adorable," I said.

"Isn't he?" George smiled, looking at the picture with awe, as if he'd just come upon it for the first time.

"He's gorgeous. He looks just like you." There was nothing more attractive than a new father smitten with his baby.

He asked about Claire, who hated him for hurting me, and about my parents, who had hated him before he hurt me, ever since his visit to the Midwest where he pitched a tent on our lawn and slept in it. He had been on his way to the jungles of Belize (adventurous like a merchant marine?). He'd had to test the equipment, he'd argued. As if I didn't know anything about suburban rebellion.

"How are your folks?" I asked. "Bet they're thrilled to be grandparents."

"Last week when Dad came by to see Max, he told me, 'He's crying just like you did when we didn't feed you.' He was laughing. I looked at him and said, 'Why didn't you feed me, Dad?' "

"What did your dad say?"

"He said I was always hungry. So what—that's normal. I was a baby. He didn't get it," George chuckled, as if it was a joke.

I touched George's shoulder. The reason he liked it here, he said, was the close proximity to the water. He'd seemed his happiest during the two weeks we'd spent on the cliffs of Jamaica, in a cabin with no electricity, when I'd mastered rock climbing, snorkeling, and peeing in the water. Not that I was Zelig. At my private high school I was voted "least likely to join a cult, most likely to start one." Yet I like loosening up. With George I was young, light, casually chic like a Ralph Lauren magazine spread. Our last night in Negril we drank Red Stripe, smoked ganja on the beach. He placed a bone ring on my ring finger in front of a blazing fire. Then we went skinny-dipping in the ocean. George was a torpedo in the water; I couldn't keep up with him. I bet that his fast swimming impressed his father.

When I was a kid, my grandparents and Aunt Shirley moved to Florida, where we'd visit every year. My father used to take us to the beach. My brothers had pale skin like my mother, even dark-haired Michael. They fried quickly in the sun, all their freckles coming together. I was the only one who could stay in the ocean with Dad all afternoon, without burning.

When I was fifteen my father had a pool built in our backyard. Every summer day it didn't rain, I could be found floating on a raft in the middle of the water. My friends didn't bother calling. If there was any sun, they knew where to find me. My mother brought out food, then retreated indoors. My brothers dabbled, dove off the diving board, threw each other off plastic rafts, then went inside. I swam and tanned and floated for hours. Even after I moved to New York, I'd make sure to come home to Michigan every August. In fact, I was going next week. I couldn't wait to wake up, run outside, and jump right in the water.

Over the years my father and I had had our best talks while he cleaned the pool and fiddled with the filter and heater. Was that why I loved swimming? My mother always said I won the gene lottery: I got her perfect eyes and my father's good feet and olive skin.

She tended to forget the nicotine addiction—another thing George and I had in common.

"Did you notice I quit smoking?" I asked him.

"I stopped six years ago," he said. "When did you give it up?"

"Awhile ago." It had only been six months; he'd won that one too.

I flashed to the day George and I swore we'd quit together. We were taking a day trip to Jones Beach in his beige Honda Civic. After six hours, I was sweating and itchy, suffering through withdrawal with serious shakes. That must have looked attractive, half nude and in a public place. Ignoring my condition, George ogled bikinis passing by. A screaming match resulted in my taking a cab back to the city for eighty dollars, stopping to buy smokes on the way. That night he came over and apologized with yellow tulips from the Korean deli, reimbursing my eighty dollars. "It's worse for you," he said as he held me. "Your dad smoked. I didn't know it would be so hard." Why was everything about fathers?

"What made you finally kick it?" he asked.

"Trying to get pregnant," I mumbled. It was the first time I had wanted to emulate my mother. How tragic it would be if my healthiest instinct turned out to be a physical impossibility.

"Really?" he smiled. "You'll be a great mother."

I was touched by his kindness, hoped it wasn't tinged with pity. Was that what I wanted from the men I used to love—permission to have what they couldn't give me? We sat down on a green bench at the water's edge. It was a hot, breezy day. I had the feeling I'd never see him again. It was my last chance. "So what happened between us?" I asked.

"Oh Sue," he said. "I was so immature and stupid and incapable back then."

I could tell he'd also been in therapy. That was why he was married to someone who sounded nice, with a cute kid and how-we-reconnected fable. Immature, stupid, and incapable wasn't exactly an apology, but it admitted guilt. It was better than his previous final words, after he'd found Diana, lost his Jane Street sublet, and called to say, "I want my bed frame back." Enraged that he'd cared more about twenty dollars' worth of wood than about my hurt feelings, I'd said, "I'll burn it on your lawn," as I hung up.

Now I added, "We were too different, in retrospect," wishing I had a cigarette.

As if to stop my crawl through our West Village wreckage, he threw out nicer images: the fancy scout knife I had bought him with the eighty dollars cab fare he returned after the beach fiasco. The black bikini I wore when we were together in Jamaica. The poem I'd scrawled in my notebook; at least I got a good poem out of the deal. He remembered the title, "Sunscreen."

"Aaron and I went to Jamaica on our honeymoon," I let slip.

"Yeah, I've been back a million times," he retaliated.

In the poem George was a bronzed fish, fluttering around the deep. He leapt off white cliffs, shouted, "Eels! Barracudas!" and brought back treasures: striped shells, brain coral. I was hiding in the shade with a stack of books I had to review. The last stanza ended, "I'll join you under the surface / after essays by an Asian feminist / or maybe I'll lend you a slow book of sadness set in Ecuador / so we can share the same journey."

Why hadn't we? I spent years unraveling the reasons he left. Right before the end, I visited him here. He drove me to the Brooklyn promenade. Holding my hand in the moonlight, he showed me a line of two-story houses on the water, and said, "Wouldn't it be amazing to live in one of those brownstones someday?"

"I didn't leave Michigan to live in Brooklyn," I said, without thinking. Nine years later I understood what my words meant. George was from Brooklyn, his wife was too. So was Diana. He'd given her a role in his play. If I'd wanted to be in his play, in Brooklyn, would I have George and his baby now?

"Her voice is full of money," Gatsby said of Daisy. Since fifth grade I had identified with Fitzgerald's "honest" narrator Nick Carraway. How strange to recast myself, even momentarily, in the role of frilly heroine in the ultimate class drama. Had I broken his heart first? No wonder I distorted the truth. George had me nailed from the start.

"It's nice to see you back in Brooklyn," he said with a wry smile.

I was glad to see George's face one more time, to say good-bye a better way, with the benefit of time, a little more wisdom, and a wedding ring.

"I'm glad you were free today," I said.

"I only missed two meetings." George smiled, looked at his watch again.

I was flattered; I still had the power to at least ruin his schedule.

The sedan returned to the archway. I hugged George, then boarded my black chariot back to Manhattan. I was exhausted, my stomach empty and growling. At home I changed into sweats and ordered a pepperoni pizza from MaMa Mia's across the street. I left out Daisy and the pizza in the version I told Aaron when he came home that night.

"The campus is on the water." I slid next to him on the couch, wishing my husband liked to swim, but he didn't. "It's kind of pretty."

Aaron put his arm around me and kissed me on the lips. "Can't see you in Brooklyn," he said.

5

Beach Boy

When Tom called to say he'd be in Michigan over Labor Day, it was clear I had old boyfriend karma. I was about to make my annual pilgrimage to the Midwest myself, staying with my family for two weeks.

"We have to get together. Let's have dinner," I told him.

Tom's timing was ideal. Aaron would only be joining me for three days, and Maria, Tom's wife of twelve years who had ordered him never to speak to me again, had just left him. I said, "Sorry about Maria." We made a date for Saturday night of the holiday weekend.

There was now no doubt in my mind that this dig through my dubious past was fate. I had unearthed my trio of ex-amours—Brad, George, and Tom—with astounding symmetry. July, August, September. Single, married, divorcing. Hell, purgatory, heaven. Seeing Tom would be wonderful, completely nonthreatening. Aaron was coming to Michigan from August 24 to 26. I asked him if he wanted to stay a few extra days to meet Tom. Surprise—no interest whatsoever.

"Do you remember who Tom is?" I tested.

"Yeah, the nice one," he answered, blowing me a kiss at the door, late for a meeting.

Sometimes I swore my husband had no idea who I was. Other times I realized he knew too much. The word Aaron retained was *nice*, since it so rarely described my old boyfriends. During my first twenty-two years as a solo player I'd avoided nice guys. You've heard of the mother/whore complex, I had the father/cad version. I couldn't be close to a male physically and emotionally at the same time. I could either lust for a loser or deeply care for someone I didn't want to sleep with. Before Aaron, Tom Stevens was the only guy I lusted for and liked at the same time.

Fellow seniors, we met during the spring of our last semester in Ann Arbor. He was the Robert Redford of campus—a blond, lithe, aloof, five-eleven, tennis-playing pre-law major with pale curly hairs all the way up his slender legs. In my hippie poet stage, I was still entranced by David, my pre-med Canadian beau and official first love. But David was long distance in more ways than I understood that balmy March.

I noticed Tom coming out of the law library a few times, holding a stack of folders and thick books. I began to study there too, to accidentally bump into him. We became friendly. I developed a secret "crunch." He'd say, "Hi Sue. How's it going?" That night I'd make myself come, thinking of pulling off his little white tennis shorts. It seemed harmless, since Mr. Suave was way out of my league lookswise.

On the weird gray Wednesday morning when I learned why David had disappeared, I sat on a corner bench in the diagonal in front of the library, sobbing uncontrollably. Tom saw me and came over.

"You okay?" he asked.

I was mortified that he'd caught me in basket-case mode, red nosed, mascara running down my cheeks, newly dumped. "I've been better." I laughed at my pathetic predicament and at Tom's timing. I couldn't possibly have looked worse. He couldn't possibly have looked hotter. It figured he'd picked this very moment for our first real conversation.

"Can't be that bad." He handed me a Kleenex from his knapsack.

"I just found out my roommate's been sleeping with my boyfriend for six months. In my apartment." I blew my nose.

"We should get you out of there," Tom said, springing to action, way ahead of me.

"I signed a lease till May. I have to watch the two of them having sex for three months." I blew my nose again. "Unless I drop out."

"No way I'm letting you drop out, my dear." He put his arm around me.

Now I got it. Turned out my tears and the "needy woman" sign on my forehead had beckoned him. Rather than scaring him off, my crisis had brought out Tom's instant brother instincts. I already had three brothers and wasn't really in the market for another. Yet since the best antidote to a two-timing loser was having an Adonis by my side, I let Tom adopt me.

He treated for double scoops of chocolate-marshmallow ice cream, my favorite, which we ate strolling around campus. Skipping classes, he bought me scented candles and bubble gum at Middle Earth, the fun leftover-from-the-sixties store. We talked about graduate school—I was planning to get my master's in English at NYU. He had been accepted to UCLA Law School. We were going in different directions, always good for drama. After a few glasses of cheap white wine at the Brown Jug, he said, "I'll walk you home." The sun was falling.

"I don't want to go home," I said. I didn't want Tom to leave.

"Then I'm coming with you," he said.

We stopped by his pad, a dumpy almost barren one-hundred-square-foot room in a house with nine other guys. (No wonder he didn't invite me to stay with him.) He grabbed clothes and books and walked me to State Street like a police escort.

At my apartment, Nicole, the boyfriend thief, wasn't around. Tom and I watched TV in my room. He insisted on staying the night. We shared my single bed like spoons, his arm around my waist. We spooned both ways three nights in a row. Aside from his protective (yet passive) arm, he didn't touch me. I went from obsessing over the guy who was screwing my roommate to obsessing over the guy who wasn't screwing me. On the fourth night I jumped him. The reality was as good as the fantasy.

Tom felt like a late Christmas present, to make up for the hideous three-way trauma. He pretty much moved in, always there yet unobtrusive. People whispered about the shirtless hunk having breakfast with Sue every morning as we ignored Nicole—no sign of my ex—and read the papers. That new gossip overshadowed the scandalous triangle, twisting the tacky story line to my benefit. It was no longer obvious to our crowd that I'd been cuckolded and was stuck for three months in a battle zone where Nicole always won. Many assumed I'd dumped Wannabe Doc for Beach Boy.

"You're still into David," Tom said one night.

"I know. I never get over anything," I admitted.

"That's why I'm apprehensive about sex."

"Get over it," I told him.

He became carefree, loose, up for anything. We did it outside in the arboretum one night, then in my orange Cutlass with a Joni Mitchell eight-track playing. Not crazy about my round-the-clock Bob Dylan, Tom was my only partner who chose to listen to a woman's voice while making love.

I drove home to West Bloomfield for the first night of Passover. Tom went to his parents' house in Troy, Michigan, ten minutes away, so he could drop by after our seder to meet my family. I sneaked him in as a friend. My parents took to him immediately, surprising since he was broke and Catholic (though his stoic cool seemed WASPy).

Even my three brothers, who used to tell my phoning suitors, "Sue doesn't like you anymore, stop calling" and hang up, unanimously gave Tom the thumbs-up. I'd won the boyfriend lottery and soon, my undergraduate diploma.

At lunch to celebrate our graduation, Tom looked at me and said, "I'm afraid you're in deeper than I am. I can't wait to get to L.A. I don't want you to get hurt."

Too late. My Beach Boy rebound had blindsided me. He'd made himself indispensable, as if I were a bird whose damaged wing he fixed—only to break it again! On the other hand, after David and my roommate, it was barely a nick. "Thanks for the warning," I told him. I spent a wild weekend with Brad (see chapter 2), then moved to New York City as soon as I could get on a plane.

I had to leave before Tom left me. David had already stained the love section of my future collection of bad confessional poetry. No guy was gonna taint my love affair with New York. Philip Roth, I'd give a few months leeway. A goy toy lawyer on his way west, who had better legs than I did? He didn't even have the balls to pretend to love me back! What fun was that? I'd graduated college—and victimhood.

Landing in the big city, I enrolled in the summer semester, went to NYU readings, starting seeing Dr. G. (who had a sliding scale for students and agreed to charge me just $20 a session), and swore I'd never move back to Michigan. David and Tom started calling again, proving that leaving was, for men, the ultimate aphrodisiac. I ignored their messages, though Tom caught me in the dorm one day.

"What's up?" he asked. I demanded to know why he was calling. "I'm thinking of driving to New York with your brothers next weekend," he threw out. "They miss you." He wanted to subject himself to a ten-hour road trip with the Three Stooges because *they* missed me? How unconscious was this guy?

"Thought you didn't want to hurt me," I taunted.

"Maybe I was afraid to get hurt," he confessed.

"Good answer," I said. "See you Friday." Nobody had ever used my brothers to get to me before; it was endearing. Besides, I was scared, lonely, and broke. A posse of big male Midwest visitors to the rescue.

They showed up at NYU's Weinstein Hall one afternoon in July. Brian, wearing a Tigers cap and my father's green scrubs, handed me a bag. It contained a bottle of magnesium citrate for constipation, Lomotil pills for diarrhea, samples of Midol, and Band-Aids—Dad's idea of a care package. Eric had grown a red beard to distinguish himself from Brian. Michael marveled that I lived without a television. The three of them took over my two-hundred-square foot dorm room, while Tom and I checked into a discounted room at the Hilton in midtown. Tom drew a heart on the little "Welcome to New York" card and slipped it in my purse.

Since the boys were underage, Tom had promised my parents he would chaperon, which he did with aplomb. For three days he led the troops on a tour of the Statue of Liberty, Empire State Building, Forty-second Street porn shops, and the *Intrepid*. By day I was toiling at the secretarial job I'd landed at a Rockefeller Center publishing house. We met for dinner at a coffee shop near my office.

"We checked out the East Village," Michael said. "Some interesting specimens down there."

"Was that guy transsexual?" Eric asked.

"Hermaphrodite." Brian took a bite from his cheeseburger.

"Ambiguous genitalia," Michael explained, chomping on a hot dog. "He had marked gynecomastia, obvious exogenous estrogen."

"Will you tell your brothers to stop diagnosing the East Village?" Tom laughed. Everything about my brothers cracked him up.

A day after Tom had driven them back to Michigan, a thirteen-inch black television set arrived from Macy's, with a card that said "To remember us." It was signed by "The Four Musketeers." When I called to say thank you, Tom asked if he could fly back for the rest of the summer. What the hell, I was new in town, I could use my own chaperon.

Tommy, as I began calling him, helped me move out of the dorm. We loaded seven garbage bags filled with my poetry books, blue jeans, perfume, and flea market lamps into a cab and unloaded them into my new $450-a-month East Twelfth Street walk-up studio. We slept on a Jennifer convertible sofa that squeaked when we fooled around. Tom had landed a low-paying summer law clerk job on the Upper East Side. At night, after my classes, we hung out in Washington Square Park, which he called "Ann Arbor on acid." I was still wearing the working-girl suits my mother had sent from Michigan; a homeless park regular took to greeting me with, "Hey, pretty clothes. What ya doin' here again?" Though broke, Tom emptied his pockets in the guy's hands, then walked fifty blocks to work the next day to save money on tokens. I read Tom my poetry.

"This is what you were put on the planet for," he flattered. "Don't ever stop writing. It's your magic." I was always a sucker for a good review. He was the first guy I trusted enough to show my rough drafts.

He was going to be a defense attorney in L.A., helping the downtrodden, which fit with my suffering artist scenario. I told myself it was just a summer fling, knowing he was going to slaughter my heart a second time when he moved out West. But I couldn't get over the immature thrill that someone so gorgeous wanted me—even on a short-term basis. I took as my banner W. H. Auden's

line: "If equal affection cannot be / let the more loving one be me."
As September loomed closer, I switched to Elizabeth Bishop's:
"The art of losing / isn't hard to master." Yet, before he left, Tom
said, "Distance is not an issue. I can't live without you."

For the next few years we scraped together enough for cheap
seats on the red-eye. When he was coming, I'd take the bus to
meet him at Kennedy Airport. We'd have passionate make-out
scenes at the gate, as if he were a soldier returning from overseas.
We'd spend the weekend in bed, playing "Beat the Chinaman"
(where we'd order in Chinese food and try to have sex before it arrived) and spooning in our sleep.

In the fall, when I told Tom I was ten days late for my period, he
flew to New York again. He said we could have the baby if I
wanted. He offered to take the bar exam in New York and mentioned marriage. I was twenty-two. It was the first time I'd ever
lived alone and I loved it. I'd landed an editorial assistant job at *The
New Yorker.* I was staying until midnight at the magazine every
night, typing my poems and first-person essays, pretending I was a
reporter on deadline for two dollars a word.

A friend gave me the number of an uptown gynecologist, Dr.
Cherry (his real name, I swear). He had four daughters and four
published books; the books cinched it. I took the first open appointment for an abortion. Tom came with me and stayed in the
waiting room.

"I was using a diaphragm," I told Dr. Cherry. I was edgy and
nervous in a little pink cotton gown. I wondered if they came in
black.

"Have you lost weight recently?" he asked. He was a nice-
looking guy, I guessed in his late fifties. I liked it that he was still
tan in October. My type: a vain, sun-worshipping writer.

"Yeah, seven or eight pounds."

"You have to have the diaphragm refitted if your weight changes,"
he said.

"Now they tell me."

"I mention that in my book *Healthy Pregnancy*," he said, writing notes into his chart.

"Who published it?" I asked, books a much more calming subject.

"Simon & Schuster."

"How many copies did it sell?"

"Forty thousand," he said, shaking his head.

"Forty thousand hardcovers is nothing to sneeze at . . ."

"My first one did better."

"Knock me out all the way," I said.

When we came back to my place, Tom wanted to talk about it and cuddle. I wanted to work, be alone. The more he loved me, the less I wanted him. I was becoming like the men I detested, recoiling from any neediness or emotion. I told Dr. G. I feared I was more masculine than feminine. I was too tough and self-sufficient to ever get married.

"So what? In your family, anything masculine was praised more," she said. "There's not a certain type who can't get married."

Even if there wasn't, every flower, book, and cute Hallmark card Tom brought me estranged us further. In seven days we turned back into brother and sister. I didn't go with him to the airport when he left for L.A. We stayed in touch sporadically, until he asked me to stop calling because it bothered Maria, his new girlfriend.

There was one Tom addendum. A few years later, he called to ask, "Are you sure it's over between us?" I said it was. A week later he and Maria announced their engagement. Though I was flattered, it seemed the most insane thing I'd ever heard, calling an old girlfriend in case she'd changed her mind, then immediately proposing to girl number two. Dr. G. disagreed. "It's all timing," she said. "When you're ready, you're ready. You go for your fantasy. If that doesn't work, you try someone available."

Her theory was that for three years Tom and I had tricked my neurosis with implausibility and literal distance. He was my sole healthy relationship because he lived three thousand miles away. With the possibility of marriage and a baby in the picture, I choked, which was starting to seem like a recurring pattern.

"Sure you don't want to meet Tom?" I tried Aaron again that night. He was leaning over his computer. "You'll like him."

He shook his head, staring at the multiple minidocuments on his screen. "Don't have time." He was in his "stay-away-from-me" mood, three months late for a script. While I was early for everything, Aaron never met a deadline he couldn't miss. "You marry your dark side," he said.

Iris Murdoch's philosophy was that "being married is the best possible way of being alone." I'd decided that Aaron had picked me because I was so self-sufficient. I was the only one he knew who, for months at a time, would stay out of his hair. Or was that the reason I'd married him?

6

I ran to the porch when Tom's car pulled into my parents' circular driveway, right on time, at six o'clock. "Tommy!" I called.

"It's Tom," he corrected with a smile, hugging me.

He was still adorable, with the same sweet yet rugged face. He'd lost some blond hair on top, and had less boyish radiance. Yet he looked trim in a Polo shirt and white cords. I was in black jeans and black sweater; black and white: we contrasted as usual.

"Your Morticia mode," he said. "You look chic, my dear."

"My dear" melted me. With his ironic detachment, the old-fashioned endearment seemed courtly, as though he were a southern gentleman. I'd forgotten how disarming he could be.

"You okay?" I asked.

"Fine," he said. "Are your folks home? I haven't seen them in years."

I took his hand and led him to my mother's kitchen, which was bigger than my entire New York apartment. It had warm pastel wallpaper, a full-sized refrigerator, matching full-size freezer and pantry. On the marble island in the middle, oversized oatmeal raisin cookies were stacked in the Lucite holder, hand painted with my parents' names: "Have a Snack with Mickey and Jack." As usual, food was everywhere—brisket on the stove, pasta and mashed potatoes on the counter, along with lamb chops, Caesar salad, and pickles. My parents were sitting at the huge mahogany table, having dinner.

"Mickey, you look the same," Tom told my mother, hugging her hello.

"Let me get you something to eat." She went for a plate.

"That's okay, we're going out," I said.

Tom shook my father's hand. "Dr. Shapiro, good to see you," he said.

"Call me Jack," my father said. "How's the L.A. law biz? I heard you left the D.A.'s office. Good, make a living. Susie says you're doing malpractice." My father was unusually chatty, as if my nostalgia for my lost youth was contagious.

"Defending doctors," Tom clarified, the surest way to Daddy's heart; no wonder Tom had wanted to come inside. (He'd become disenchanted with the downtrodden around the time I'd switched from poetry to slick magazine spreads.)

Tom was as excited to see my parents as he was to see me. He used to be part of the family. They loved him, saw him as a clean-cut, modest man who had put himself through school, like my father. Not to mention their eternal gratitude that he'd saved me from my breakup-triangle catastrophe during our senior year of college.

"Will you at least have a cup of coffee?" my mother asked.

"I'd love to." He sat down.

Tom wasn't in a hurry, letting her pour him a tall cup of gourmet coffee. I took a diet soda and sat down. Having recently gone reconciliation-crazy, I certainly was in no position to step on his reunion fantasy. He and my father exchanged tales about HMO assholes while I looked at Tom's white corduroys. They had been the cause of a fight one December, seventeen years earlier. We were getting ready for a holiday party. "You can't wear white cords in the winter," I'd said. They seemed out of date, uncool, too collegiate for the big city.

"Who cares what I wear?" he'd asked.

"Come on. Please change. For me."

"You're a bitch," he'd said, putting on black jeans.

"You're right," I'd said, glad I won.

It was superficial, but a partner was a mirror. Over the years, my clothes had reflected each lover's preference. (I'd dressed preppy for Tom, wearing khakis, cashmere sweaters, and the pearls my mother bought me.) Thus I felt justified in insisting that my male cohorts wear faded blue jeans, flannel shirts, and cowboy boots. My phantom lover was the Marlboro Man who, Dr. G. pointed out, dressed the exact opposite of a suit like my father.

"How's everything else?" my mother asked Tom, offering him milk and sugar.

"Getting divorced," he said quietly, though I'd already told them.

"Happens to a lot of people," my father said, eating a lamb chop.

"I bet nobody in your family is divorced," Tom said, pouring a little milk and stirring.

"His sister Shirley was sort of divorced." My mother put another lamb chop on my father's plate. "After she was widowed."

"What?" I was stunned. As far as I knew, Shirley, my father's late sister, had been married to my Uncle Frank for forty-five years. "I didn't know Shirley was ever married to anybody but Frank."

"Oh yeah," my dad said. "This was before Frank."

"When?"

"When she was eighteen," my mother said.

I remembered a photograph of Shirley as a thin, sexy, raven-haired girl on her tenement's fire escape. Aside from me, she was the only other dark-haired woman on either side of the family. "Who did she marry?" I was intrigued.

"Shirley married Ira Katzenberg, who was a brilliant teacher," my mother said. "But his family turned out to be meshuggeneh."

"That means nutsy," I translated for Tom.

"It sounds like it means nutsy," he said.

"After two years Ira got sick. He was dying." She took the lamb chops my father had finished, chewing on the bones.

"Inoperable brain tumor," my father said. "Shirley was going to have to pay his medical bills, so she divorced him so she wouldn't be responsible."

"Was Ira upset?" I asked.

"No, he told her to divorce him. He insisted." She took a shrimp cocktail from the refrigerator and put it on the table near Tom. "Sure you don't want anything to eat?"

"That's okay," I told her. "We're going out."

"Did she still love him?" Tom asked.

My mother nodded. "She took care of him until he died. She was destroyed. But while she was mourning, Ira's family told her she had to marry Ira's single brother, Ezra, who was short and smoked cheap, smelly cigars."

"Why should she marry Ezra?" I asked.

"Jewish law," my father said. "The Torah said that a widow married her deceased husband's single brother."

"What year was this? 1605?" Tom asked. He took a shrimp and dipped it in cocktail sauce.

"Early fifties," my mother told him. "Can you believe it?" I could tell she liked this story. "Anyway, Shirley said she's not marrying Ezra. She was already going with Frank 'cause he made her laugh. But everyone was afraid of the Katzenbergs—they had mystic rabbis from Russia on their side. If you offended them, they'd put a curse on you. They said Shirley had to be divorced from Ira, which she wasn't."

I was getting confused. "I thought you said she got divorced from Ira."

"She got American divorced," my mother said. "She needed a Jewish divorce certificate—a Get—or else she was a widow who had to marry Ezra. So her father, Susie's grandpa Harry, went to a special rabbi he knew."

"No, he didn't," my father said. "Uncle Tudras did."

"Right. Uncle Tudras came from Odessa, he was very well connected," she said. "He went to visit a special rabbi he knew in Brooklyn."

"No, you're wrong," my father said. "It was on Eastern Parkway."

"So you tell the story." She took their dishes to the sink. "Mickey, you always do this."

"Someone finish the story," I said, pouring more diet soda.

"Okay," my father said. "Uncle Tudras had a secret meeting with a big-shot Hasid on Eastern Parkway, Rabbi Rosen. For weeks Rosen and all his disciples went through hundreds of volumes of the Kabala."

"I know, it's Jewish mysticism," Tom said to me.

"They found an obscure passage about divorce that applied." My father was speaking slowly for emphasis; he liked this story too. "They sent Shirley to the cemetery on the eve of Rosh Chodesh, a special Friday night when there was a full moon, with twelve Kabalist rabbis from Lublin. They made Shirley stand on the grave."

"The twelve rabbis stood around her," my mother said.

I pictured a swarm of male spies in long dark coats carrying Shirley across a graveyard at midnight. I imagined it was me standing there.

"They all had beards down to their *pupiks*," my mother added. "Tell that to your therapist."

"*Pupik* is a belly button," I told Tom and he laughed.

"The rabbis said a Hebrew prayer, divorcing a dead man." My father laughed too.

"She got the Get and gave it to the Katzenbergs, who couldn't argue with Tudras's rabbi," my mother said.

"Then she married Frank," my father added.

"He was a nut too." My mother shrugged.

"Meshuggeneh," Tom said, pronouncing it wrong.

"For forty-five years Frank was either unemployed or thin," my mother said. "He couldn't do both. Either three hundred pounds and rich or one hundred seventy and poor, with the lights turned off 'cause he didn't pay his bills."

"Nothing good ever happened to Shirley." My father shook his head.

"Maybe she should have married Ezra," Tom said.

"I wonder what would have happened." My mother poured Tom more coffee.

It took another half hour to drag Tom out of there. Dad, who had weirdly discovered blue jeans in his old age, walked us to the door. He wasn't worried that his thirty-nine-and-a-half-year-old married daughter was having dinner with a dashing ex-lover. Nothing seemed inappropriate. Dad used to greet me and my dates at the door in boxers and T-shirt, his big belly sticking out, six-inch cigar in his mouth. Now he was sociable and charming, spinning tales of his loopy Jewish relatives. I missed his territorial male rage, and felt old, as if everything had been neutered. It must not have occurred to Dad, now sixty-eight, that I could be doing anything racy with Tommy.

"Great cords," I said as we got into Tom's father's beige sedan.

"I knew you'd like them." He grinned widely, like a four-year-old stealing candy.

"Did you save them just for this moment?"

"Yes." He laughed.

"They're still horrendous."

We cruised around aimlessly, Motown blasting on the radio, singing to "Heard It Through the Grapevine," the Dee-troit anthem, which had been playing since I'd left.

"Your parents are so great," he said. "I could talk to them forever."

"I couldn't wait to move out at sixteen, but the last few years I've had such a good time visiting Michigan."

"Because your brothers all moved out," he said. "You're finally an only child."

"Is that why?"

"How are your brothers doing?" he asked.

"Brian and Eric are married with kids."

"I bet they're great fathers. Strong like your dad, but warm like your mother."

I'd never thought of it that way.

"I heard Mike's in Chicago," he said. "I can't believe the little guy's a doctor now."

"A cardiologist," I said.

"Heart doctor." Tom was delighted. "As you would say, a good metaphor."

We were both the oldest of four, the caretakers, probably why we didn't already have broods of our own.

"Did you tell Claire to call me?" Tom asked. She was designing a boutique on Rodeo Drive. When I'd heard Tom was single again, I gave her his number.

"That's right, she said you two had coffee. How was it?"

"Friends," he said.

"I got the vibe she likes you," I pushed. "You should take her out to dinner."

"It would be too bizarre to date your best friend." He shook his head.

"Not attracted?" I asked.

"Are you kidding? She's always been hot." He paused. "But I want to be able to come by and say hi to Mickey and the doc."

"You can always," I said, wishing he'd wind up with Claire. I was a faithful middle-aged married woman, nobody would mind. I thought of Shirley divorcing a dead man, then refusing his brother. "She should have married Ezra," Tom had said.

Over dinner at Beau Jacks, I chronicled my book's rejection, the trying-to-have-a-baby blues, reunions with Brad and George, fights with my elusive husband.

"I think Aaron wants a long-distance marriage." I finished my chicken and picked at Tom's salad. I always ate more than he did. "In the last two months, he's been to L.A. three times, then spent a week in Seattle to meet a producer he doesn't even like."

"He wants to be a success for you." Tom pushed his croutons to my side of his plate. "A guy doesn't think he deserves a woman if he's not successful."

"Don't be insightful. Be on my side." I ate them with my fingers.

"I like the sound of Aaron," he said. "I see him as a Jewish me."

He wasn't all wrong. Aaron was a food martyr too, deciding what on his plate I'd like, unconsciously saving it for me. Like Tom, Aaron had a kid sister. They knew how to look out for a little girl, pretending they weren't being protective. They were the only guys my dad and brothers approved of, which, I hated to admit, meant they were the only guys I could have married.

"What happened with Maria?" I asked.

"Didn't work out," he said.

In the best picture we'd taken, I had a cigarette in my hand. I wore a purple sweater and a frantic expression. Next to me was this hunky blond guy in a beige sweater, looking serene.

"I moved out. Gave her the house," was all he said. He remained Mr. Mystery, repressing as much as I was spilling heedlessly.

We fought for the check. I grabbed it. "It's on me. I ate half your food and shared my entire neurotic psychosexual history," I said. "Sorry I'm so nuts."

"You seem together, my dear," he said. "On your one-to-ten neurotic scale, I give you a two."

"Ten's the most neurotic?" I asked.

He nodded.

"You're crazy. I'm way up there."

"No," he insisted. "You're married to a good man, doing what you love. You're fine," he said, like a kind storefront fortune teller. When he dropped me off, back at my parents' house, he kissed my cheek, but declined to come in.

In my old pink bedroom, surrounded by pink carpet, pink wallpaper, and pink stereo, I took my emotional temperature. My heart felt quiet; how uncharacteristic. In my writing workshop the worst insult was "There's no blood here." That meant you didn't go deep enough. Not dishonest, just too on the surface, my tendency. I hadn't asked myself or Tom the right questions, blowing my chance to find cathartic meaning in our reconnection. It was too late. Or maybe it wasn't.

I called Tom the next morning and asked, "What are you doing tonight?"

"I have a family dinner. Should I come by late?"

"Sure." Seeing each ex one time was a reunion. Twice was asking for trouble. "Want to take a walk around the lake with me? It's exactly one mile. I walk four or five times around every day." Nervous, I was talking too much. "My mother comes with me sometimes. But she doesn't like to walk in the dark. She thinks you could stumble or get hurt." Tom was an insomniac, like me. At least he used to be.

"See you at midnight," he said.

Waiting in the kitchen at 11:45 on Sunday night, I heard my father turning on the burglar alarm. "Don't," I stopped him. "I'm going out."

"Where?" asked my dad, in T-shirt and boxers, looking confused.

"Tom's coming over. We're going for a walk." That sounded really strange.

"Okay," he mumbled, unfazed. "Is Tommy okay?"

"I don't know."

"Divorcing. Hates his job. Give Tommy Eric's e-mail address," he instructed.

My brother Eric, who'd forsaken the family business of medicine, had become a freelance techie for Apple. (Nobody in the family worked well with others.) Dad was trying to find his married daughter's old lover a new profession. For the Shapiros, worry transcended social etiquette. And Tom was forever Tommy.

My mother came downstairs, wearing her long pink silk nightgown and robe set.

"She's taking a walk with Tommy," my father told her.

"So don't turn on the alarm," she said.

"Did you get them?" he eyed her sheepishly.

She took a big cookie from under the Lucite holder and put it in his mouth. "Just one," she said. "You're on a diet."

"Then why did you get my favorite?" he mumbled, chewing happily.

"Forty-six years and he's still surprised I get his oatmeal raisin cookies." She handed him a napkin. "Doesn't mean you have to eat five a day."

"Maybe it was the dowry," my father said. "I bet the Katzenbergs didn't want to give Shirley back her dowry."

"If she married Ezra, the Katzenbergs would get to keep it," my mother said. Then she went up the stairs, pink lace trailing.

"Who you marry changes everything," my father said, following.

Tom appeared ten minutes later, in jeans, sneakers, and down vest. It was cold for the start of September. The temperature had plunged into the forties. I grabbed my father's blue peacoat and big flashlight.

"We don't need a flashlight," Tom said. But I took it anyway, as there were no streetlights on and you couldn't see a step in front of you. As we walked outside, he changed his mind, took the flashlight from me, and turned it on. It was high power, illuminating the driveway and the street.

"How was dinner with your family?" I asked as we turned at the end of the driveway. Freezing, I wanted to give up my brilliant take-a-midnight-walk idea. "It got chilly."

"Good." Half a block later, he said, "I brought you something." He pulled a pin joint from his pocket, lit it, and handed it to me.

"Thanks." Even his joints were tidy. I sucked in deeply a few times. It was strong. I handed it to him. "What happened with Maria?" My parents could tell an ancient divorce fable, sidestepping his real-life problem while somehow making him feel better. Literal-minded till the end, I needed it spelled out more. "Tommy, you have to tell me."

"You're the only one who calls me that," he said.

"What happened?"

"Nothing. She wanted to sing. I supported her. Gave her money for lessons, to cut a CD. She fell for a guy in the band."

It was easier for him to tell me getting high in the dark; he didn't have to look at me. "Didn't she have a kid?"

"We have a son, Peter. I adopted him when he was five. His natural father wasn't really around. She was raising him alone."

"I'm sorry it didn't work out," I said, worried that all men preferred wounded birds.

"It's okay," he told me.

Why was it okay? I was annoyed. I inhaled slowly, holding smoke in too long, coughing. "Why did you give her the house? Did you give her the furniture too?" When I finished the joint, I stepped on the tiny leftover roach and put it in my pocket. This was Middle American suburbia, after all. Any trace of drugs could cause a Bloomfield scandal.

"Where are you living?" I asked him. You could hear crickets, a dog barking. It was spooky out here this late. "What's your new place like?" I inched closer and accidentally bumped into him as we rounded the cul-de-sac. In the past it would have been intentional, a ploy so he'd put his arm around me, kiss me, ravage me outside in the woods for kicks, like he used to. I had the vague recollection we once did it against a tree. When you wed, old attractions were supposed to dissipate, dammit. Yet I felt attracted to him and quickly moved away.

"You okay?" he asked, veering toward the opposite curb.

"That stuff was strong." I inched back, took the flashlight. Had we really done it against a tree? Who did I used to be and why couldn't I be her anymore?

"My new place is a dump." He walked faster; it was hard to keep up. "Just a bed and a laptop."

He never had been big on possessions. When he moved into my East Village studio that summer, he only took up two hangers and a shelf in the closet. He prided himself on traveling light, giving things away.

"Why don't you get yourself a decent place?" I asked.

"Can't afford it," he said. "I gave notice at work. I hate lawyers."

My father had picked up on that one, guy telepathy. Like Tommy, Dad had been the only one in his family to finish graduate school. He knew how much it meant. His sister, Shirley, wasn't even allowed to take college classes. It seemed her life was determined by which husband she chose. Yet maybe not having a career she loved was what had ruined her.

I pictured Tommy in an empty L.A. apartment, deserted by his wife and son. No job to wake up for every morning, no colleagues to talk to, no paycheck. I felt a shooting pain in my chest. I was having trouble breathing, my bra too tight. Tears welled up. Getting high speed-walking in the dark with a gorgeous ex-boyfriend was dangerous, no wonder. I was going into cardiac arrest. Could it be an anxiety attack? Probably just empathy. I was relieved we were in the dark, he couldn't see. A few steps behind him, I wiped my eyes. It was half a block before I felt the pain subside.

"Why did you give her the house?" I hated knowing that he was broke and alone.

"I wanted Peter to have somewhere to come home to," he said as we passed by my house, now on our second mile. "He's going to USC in the fall."

"Are you paying his entire tuition?" I asked. Tom nodded yes. I wanted to order him to stop, the way I'd ordered him to change out of those white corduroy pants. On our one-to-ten neurotic scale, he was off the charts. Sometimes I thought that he was the emotional Jewish poet and I was the stoic WASP inside.

"He's my son," he said. "He was five when I married her. I'm the only father he's known. It's not his fault. He's devastated."

Be selfish, I wanted to shout, like I taught myself to be. He wasn't at all angry. Was this what he'd come back for, so I could feel his rage for him? Along with rage, I felt guilty. If I would have married Tom, he wouldn't be getting divorced now. I wasn't the type to divorce, not even a dead man. I would have told the Katzenbergs to go screw themselves, along with all the rabbis.

Overwhelmed with worry and sadness, I couldn't bear to see my one-time tower of strength become human before my eyes. The one guy in the world who didn't destroy me when we split was breaking my heart now, seventeen years late.

"Peter is seventeen now," he added.

Something about the number seventeen jarred me. If we had gone through with it, we would have had a seventeen-year-old too. I'd blocked it out for years. The memory had only surfaced recently, when the fertility specialist asked if I'd been pregnant before. I couldn't believe I had erased this from my mind and body so completely. I hadn't even paid for it, Tom did.

"Ever think about if we would have kept the baby?" I ventured.

"Try not to."

"I'm sorry," I said.

"Stop saying you're sorry."

"Not for Maria but . . . if I ever hurt you."

"Shut up," he said, chuckling.

How strong-minded, brave, and sure of everything I was in my twenties. I was jealous of my old self. Especially now, when taking a walk with an old boyfriend almost killed me. When we came to my house again, he stopped and said, "It's late."

"Not that late," I said. Tom once swore that he'd do anything for me. Would he do it one more time, alter history? If I got pregnant, I'd keep the baby this time. "Let's go around the block again."

"We've been around the block, my dear," he told me, walking to his car.

"Please, don't go," I begged.

He opened the door, he wasn't kidding. "I've gotta get home." He turned on the engine, locked the doors. I knocked on the window, he rolled it down.

"If you're short on cash . . ." I said.

"I'm not," he cut me off. "It was nice to see you."

"Will you call Claire? Please?" Out of guilt, I was offering him another wife. To replace Maria. To replace me.

"I'm not calling Claire." He rolled up the window.

I stood there, watching his car pull away. He was an emissary, dropping off a ghost I didn't want to keep. Two ghosts, actually. I'd had two abortions, one with David when I was nineteen, one with Tommy when I was twenty-two. At least I figured out what the catch was, what God wanted me to see: I wasn't a helpless victim of bad boyfriends or a malfunctioning body. I'd refused to have a baby twice, with no regrets. I'd become the woman I'd wanted to be—the antimother of the world, a modern Medea. The opposite of Mickey.

Inside the house I locked the front door and turned on the burglar alarm. High and wired, I went down to my father's den. Sitting at his desk, I turned on his Apple. Dad had showed me how to get my e-mail using his "guest." When it came to computers, I was always a guest. The first e-mail was from Aaron. "How's Tommy?" he asked. Interesting. Not "How was seeing Tom?" As if he knew something was wrong.

"Okay," I typed in and sent.

Aaron must have been right at his computer because "You've got mail" rang. "A one-word answer? That bad?" he asked.

I clicked to the next one. It was my student, HOTCHICK66, always good for a laugh. She'd been e-mailing me some pretty decent music reviews she'd sold to John, my editor friend at *The New York Press*. On the bottom she'd type the word *THANKS* ten times in caps. Yet this time she wrote that she was having a "bummer summer" because her boyfriend had moved back to Buffalo. She was thinking about dropping out of school to move back there with him. Oh no!

"You can't drop out now. Finish your degree," I instructed her. "After you graduate, then decide. You can't give a man that much power over you." I was always brilliant with other people's lives.

Next were two notes from *New York Times* editors whom I hadn't heard from in six months. They were like boyfriends—they didn't want you until you went away. I wanted to make a note to call them. Looking for a pen in my father's desk drawer, I found half a pack of Marlboros. I stared at them.

Everyone on my father's side had serious lifelong nicotine addictions. Shirley, who'd died young, of breast cancer, had been a heavy smoker. His mother had died of breast cancer too. He was a cancer doctor who couldn't save his own mother or sister.

My father quit smoking ten years ago, but Mom said he'd been sneaking cigarettes lately. He denied it, but she could smell the smoke on his breath. An item in the neighborhood newsletter had said someone had been secretly stashing empty Marlboro packs in other people's garbages. "We have a Marlboro Man in our midst," it read.

I took one from his pack, smelled it. I turned the computer off, afraid Aaron would catch me through the screen. I hadn't had a cigarette in thirteen months, the longest I'd ever quit: 396 days clean. I found matches, lit it, sucked the smoke in. It felt really good, dirty. The only time I could quit was when I thought I could have a baby. To clean my womb, reclaim my femininity.

I feared there were only two kinds of women: healthy nurturers, like my mother, with her bright red hair, too much food, and adoring family. Then there was the exotic, raven-haired Shirley, who smoked, drank, chose the wrong husbands, and couldn't bear children, her life ending so tragically.

"You're just like Shirley," my father told me.

"Jack! You're wrong," my mother hit his arm. "She is not!"

Ultimately, neither woman was my role model. I started smoking at thirteen, emulating my father, who chain-smoked while he worked here, in his den, surrounded by hundreds of hardcover books: World War II, medicine, Jewish history. I found the thin blue anthology of poems he used to read me. It was hidden in a corner on the highest row. I ran my fingers over it. "I have a little shadow that goes in and out with me . . ."

When I finished the cigarette, I lit another. I'd read there was a smoking gene, and that one's method of self-destruction was genetic.

"Of course you want to be like him," Dr. G. had once said. "He had all the power."

I finished the rest of my father's pack, having no power over anything.

7

The morning Aaron left for Asia I watched him pack. He spread out his travel clothes, work, and toiletries across the floor of the Bat Cave, then stuffed everything into his suitcase. As usual, he was frantic and late; the car was already downstairs. He shouted phone numbers at me, handed me checks he forgot to put in the bank, and kissed me good-bye quickly, missing my lips.

He'd just taken a writing job on an animated series about aliens for FOX-TV. Good side: The producers swore he'd never have to be in L.A. Bad side: The animation was done in Korea, where they were sending him for three weeks. It was the longest we'd be apart since our wedding. The money was too good to pass up, he said. I couldn't argue. The fertility tests and specialists cost thousands more than our insurance covered and my current career consisted of one three-hundred-word assignment: the review of a Holocaust memoir, just what every depressed freelancer needed.

I thought it would be relaxing to have the place to myself, without his stuff everywhere. I could do anything I wanted, write for forty-eight hours straight without showering, go on a bender. I wound up reading about Auschwitz till 5 A.M., ordering in food to keep me awake. I had bad dreams about Nazis when I slept at all, lost track of days. I was turned around without him.

It was a cold, quiet end of September. Aside from teaching Monday and Wednesday evenings, the lone event on my calendar was Claire's fortieth birthday party on Friday. Of course it was scheduled for the same night Aaron was returning home. But there was no way I could miss Claire's soiree. She'd been my closest comrade since I was born (four months after her), my doppelgänger. We always celebrated our birthdays together. I pictured potential scenarios.

After a twenty-hour flight, Aaron would be pissed off if I mentioned a party; he hated parties. When he came home, I'd kiss him, hear a few Korean alien stories, then I'd sneak uptown. Or I'd go to Claire's early for an hour and rush home to be here when he arrived. I wished he'd postpone his return by one day. When he e-mailed to say he had switched his flight to one day later, on Saturday, I felt guilty. I was a bad wife for wanting to go to Claire's party more than I wanted to greet him. My mother would have been waiting at home for my father, sweating over a brisket. No, my mother wouldn't be waiting, she'd never let him out of her sight for that long.

A fortieth birthday was atrocious enough, but Claire had split up with Hans, the German film director she'd lived with for two years, because he wouldn't cough up a ring. (Or the rent. Or stay in the same country for three weeks.) She gave up their Chelsea sublet, made a bonfire of his stuff, and bought her own two-bedroom apartment uptown. She was in mourning, doing construction, having a midlife crisis and a counterphobic urge to snag a replacement groom. I swore I'd bring drinks, presents, and single men.

"The single men are the presents," Claire said.

The party would be a good distraction from concentration camps and missing Aaron. I called as many unattached males as I could find. Luckily, in New York, most people I knew were single or on the verge of destroying relationships.

Late Thursday I finished reading the Holocaust book, a posthumous memoir by an Auschwitz survivor who had blocked out the evil he witnessed in the camps. Fifty years later he dredged it up. After completing the memoir, he'd had a heart attack and died. His memory killed him. I was enrapt, not about the atrocities of the Third Reich, but with the lines debating whether he should have relived what he experienced. The author was issuing a warning: Don't look back, the past can kill you.

Getting assigned this book right now was an omen, I decided. I was big on omens. My review focused on the dilemma, the treacherous deep-sea dive of memory, the twisted search for vanished footsteps, the perils of digging too deep. It came out long but poetic. I was proud, e-mailing it to my editor on Friday morning.

I ran out for champagne and wine, then picked up Claire's present, a purple pashmina, like the one Aaron had bought me for Hanukkah last year. Purple was Claire's favorite; she called it "the color of schizophrenia." At home I checked AOL to see if Aaron had left Asia yet. No Aaron, but there was a message from my *New York Times Book Review* editor, responding to my piece. One word: *asinine.*

I usually ignored his criticism, but this time I was shattered. I reread my three hundred words. He was right. It was vague, incoherent. I'd left out specifics. God was in the details, I always hammered into my students, a review was a news story. I should take my own class. I deleted the memory mumbo-jumbo, replaced it with facts. I rewrote the lead, but stubbornly kept the end: "After completing the memoir, he had a heart attack and died, as if his memory had killed him." I e-mailed the revised review and then jumped in the shower. When I got out, I found a further critique of my critique.

"IT DID NOT!" my editor responded. "The book was published in France in 1996. He died in 1999, THREE YEARS LATER."

How was I supposed to know that the book had been published

in France three years earlier? So memory didn't kill him after all. I
was relieved. I rewrote the end. When I looked up it was 8:06 P.M.
Damn! I was due at Claire's at eight. I blew dry my hair, threw on
a tight black sweater with Wonderbra, tight black jeans, and high-
heeled boots, which I'd bought myself. (It was too tacky to wear
the slingbacks I'd stolen from Claire to her party.)

I gathered champagne, wine, gift, coat, gloves, purse, and umbrella; I couldn't carry everything. I usually had Aaron to help, I
needed his extra hands. I locked the door, unsteady and flustered,
like I'd forgotten something. Outside, it was cold, windy, and raining. I'd never get a taxi.

"Taxi!" I yelled to the cab letting a guy off in front of my building.
What luck! I ran for it like a high-heeled bag lady, barreled inside,
and told the driver Sixty-fifth Street and Park Avenue. Though
Claire was doing incredibly well as an architect at a chichi SoHo
firm, her parents helped with the down payment of her swanky
apartment. I was jealous. If I was single at forty, I wondered if my
parents would have helped me buy my own place.

I laid the umbrella and bags on the seat and calmed down. I used
to love parties; this shouldn't be so hard. Taking off my gloves I
saw what I'd forgotten: my diamond wedding ring. Oh no, I wasn't
wearing it. Or the watch Aaron gave me. I'd taken them off before
I showered and put them on the nightstand in the bedroom, the
left one, next to his side of the bed. I meant to put them back on. I
wanted the driver to turn back around. But it was late and Claire
was going to kill me. I could barely walk in these high boots, let
alone sprint back upstairs for my ring.

As we sped up Park Avenue, I stared at my empty finger. It felt
like I'd left a friend behind. I must have been overidentifying with
Claire, feeling alone on her birthday. I didn't want to rub it in that
I was married and she wasn't. I had invited so many eligible men to
the party, I must have unconsciously desired to be single again. No

wonder; lately I'd had the restrictions of marriage but no benefits—no baby, no companionship, no warm body beside me in bed.

When I arrived at Claire's, twenty people were mingling about, most of them men. Who were these guys? I recognized a few—I'd invited them.

"You're here!" Claire rushed out of the kitchen and hugged me, taking my bags.

"Sorry I'm late. You look skinny." I kissed her and ran my hand over her black cashmere dress. "You've been working out!"

"To spite Hans, the jerk. He e-mailed me from Australia on my fortieth. Can you believe it? No present."

"We burned all his stuff," I reminded her. "And accused his grandparents of war crimes."

"So? He could have sent flowers."

"There's a lot of new men here," I commented.

"I know. They started coming right at eight." She took my bottles into the kitchen and inspected me. "Nice Wonderbra boobs. High boots? Very sexy. I was hoping you'd wear my black slingbacks. They're Prada, you know. Don't I get visitation rights? Ms. Downtown Bohemian has good taste. You owe me big. Where's Aaron?"

"Stuck in Korea till tomorrow. He sends his love."

"Why are you so late? It's nine thirty!" She took my coat to the bedroom. I followed.

"My *Times* editor hated my review, called it 'asinine.' I loused up the part on memory."

"Didn't we all?" she laughed. "Doesn't my place look good?"

"It looks fabulous." I scanned the high ceilings, minimalist decor, and black-and-white photography on the walls. Claire had great taste—except in men.

"Maybe we should have invited more women?" she asked.

"Nah," we both said.

"How was seeing Tommy in Michigan?" she asked. "He's still in love with you."

"He is not. You should call him again."

"He lives in L.A. and he's too nice for me." Since Claire was a charter member of the father/cad club, I agreed. "What's with seeing all your old boyfriends?" she asked.

"Infertility crisis, I think. I haven't touched any of them. Just talking." I brushed my hair in her mirror. "About what went wrong."

"Does it help?"

"Makes it worse," I replied.

"Did you call that fertility specialist I told you about?"

"I saw him and three others. Nothing's working."

"I'm sorry," she said, hugging me.

"Open your gift. You might hate it. I can take it back."

"You can remeet my exes, if it would be easier." She ripped open the box, pulled out the pashmina, and wrapped it around herself like a movie star swathed in mink. "Are you crazy? It's divine. My color, schizophrenic. Who's Gary? Kind of sexy."

"Friend of Aaron's. Writes for Letterman. Forty-two, never been married."

"What's wrong with him? Tell me now," she said as Gary walked in.

"Where's Aaron?" he asked.

"Stuck in Korea another day." I put my arm around her. "You met my friend Claire. Another Michigan girl."

"I did have that pleasure." Gary smiled at her and took in her short dress and crisscross hose. Good sign.

"Susie's my oldest friend in the world," Claire said. (Only my parents and Claire called me Susie.) "We were friends before we were born." She was tipsy. "Our mothers were pregnant together four times in a row."

"And we survived to tell the story." I gave her my "You can shut up now" smile.

Gary smiled back blankly, like it was a joke he didn't get. It was the truth. Even the offspring's gender matched, our three brothers the same ages. Claire and I were bonded by our inadequacy, our years of therapy trying to shrug off the overwhelming pressure to be like our mothers. Or was it guilt that we didn't have to be?

"Our goal is to be pregnant together once," Claire chirped, adding, "I need another drink. So do you." She led us back to the living room and whispered, "Gary seems smart, don't ya think?"

"Mentioning pregnancy before the first date?" I shook my head. "Why don't you just throw a grenade at him?"

"Did you see Paul?"

That was the grenade. "Paul?" Don't tell me she was still in lust with our college pal, who broke her heart sophomore year and returned every three years to repeat the agony.

"He's been calling." She poured herself more champagne.

I poured a diet soda. "You're not going to . . ." I started to say as Paul walked up to me.

"Sue. Hi. How are you? I loved your article on Brad's book."

"Hey Paul, what's going on?" I lit a cigarette.

"Have some champagne." Claire handed him a glass, then left. A dozen single guys in the living room and she was hiding in the kitchen. Nobody would have guessed I'd be wed and she'd be single. She was the wife material. Though we had the same height, dark eyes, and hair, she cooked, wore size six designer dresses, and went to synagogue on the High Holidays. I was the downtown neurotic feminist in torn jeans and therapy. How was I married?

"Brad said you quit smoking." Paul took my cigarette and put it out in a beer bottle.

"Hey!" I punched his arm. "We graduated twenty years ago. That's not cute anymore."

"You have to see my new place," he said. "Seventy-fifth and Fifth. Marble floors in all three bathrooms."

"What do you need three bathrooms for?" I asked.

"He can pee a little in each one," Claire interjected, flitting by with a cheese-and-cracker plate.

"We have the same decorator," Paul said. "My apartment's prewar too, twenty-five hundred square feet."

Our college crowd, which had always been ridiculously competitive, had now descended to dueling over apartments. Paul's cell phone rang. "Downtown we maim people who bring cell phones to parties," I said, loudly. Paul was oblivious.

"Where are you?" he said into his tiny silver machine.

"Nice party," Gary ambled over. He was Aaron's only single, straight, employed male friend; I stole him for parties. "I was hoping to see Aaron."

"Everything got switched," I said.

"Checking your stock tips?" Claire teased Paul about the cell. "Are you worth more or less than you were ten minutes ago?" She swung into the kitchen again.

"He's coming by," Paul told me.

"Who?"

"Brad," he said.

"What?" I choked on my diet soda, which dribbled down my sweater.

"College friend of ours," Paul filled Gary in. "On his book tour. Did Howard Stern's show yesterday. He was hysterical, talking about animal copulation."

"Why is Brad coming?" I asked, trying to stay calm.

"He was supposed to do a TV show in Texas, but his flight was canceled. That was him, at the airport. I told him to come by." Paul was smiling, as if this was good news. Too many plane flights changing around. "We had dinner with Claire last week. Didn't she tell you?"

"Who had dinner?"

"Me, Claire, and Brad," Paul said.

"Excuse me for a second." I marched into the kitchen, where I found Claire putting mixed nuts into a bowl. "Why didn't you tell me you had dinner with Paul and Brad? Speaking of mixed nuts." I dumped my soda in the sink. She poured me a tall glass of champagne.

"I meant to tell you. The next day I had that oral surgery, couldn't talk. I had dinner plans with Paul. Brad was in town, so Paul brought him too. I can't believe how much Paul's calling again." The doorbell rang and she ran for it.

Her oral surgery alibi checked out, but she could have e-mailed. Best friend rules mandated that she'd warn me if Brad was in town. I finished the glass and felt tingly. Or perhaps not. I'd been married five years and hadn't seen Brad in a decade, except for our recent lunch interview. There might be a statute of limitations on exes. My time to keep them out of circulation had expired. Claire was single, Paul was single, Brad was single. Tommy was single. I wasn't single.

Downing the rest of the bottle, I leaned on the kitchen counter. I could get over an innocent dinner—Claire and Paul, with Brad coming unexpectedly. Yet now Brad was in her life—he was coming to her apartment. It was wrong! He was mine, one of the top-five heartbreaks of all time, an important part of my psychodrama, ex-lover number one. I was finished with him. I had already reconquered George (number two) and Tom (number three). I was currently making emotional preparations to retackle number four. My friends couldn't flippantly resurrect number one without my permission. He was repetitious, out of sequence, confusing my outline. Yet I couldn't make a scene at Claire's Find-a-Husband party.

In the living room, I tried to decide whether I should go to the bathroom and crawl into a ball by the toilet for the rest of the night, or go home and be depressed for ten hours, waiting for my husband, where I belonged. Before I could choose, Brad walked in. He came over to me. I waved, no biggie, sloshed out of my brains.

"Hi Sue. My flight was canceled," he said. "Everything's been switched."

"I heard."

"I was on Howard Stern. Went well." He looked better than last time, his hair a bit longer. For me he looked like a marine. For Claire's party, he was hot. I lit a cigarette.

"Smoking?" He looked disappointed.

Who was he to be keeping track?

"Where's your wedding ring?" he asked.

"Having it resized," I lied. The last thing Brad would know about was wedding rings.

"Why are you smoking?" he said.

Because I can't have a baby anyway, I didn't say. "Why are you asking?" Luckily my friend Dirk walked by.

"Dirk, hi. Have you met Brad Wentworth? He wrote *Primal Power*."

"Read about it in *Salon*." Dirk nodded. "Sounds interesting."

"Dirk's an editor from *Vanity Fair*," I said, ashes falling on my sweater. I rubbed them in. Why was my sleeve wet?

"I'm doing some freelance writing," Brad said.

Brad was now a freelance writer too. I went to the kitchen to throw up. Opening the window, I sucked in some air.

"Paul's flirting with my friend Neeta!" Claire rushed in.

"Please tell me you're not into Paul again," I said.

"I thought you stopped drinking," she said.

Oh yeah, I hadn't had a drink in over a year. No wonder I was this dizzy. "Why didn't you tell me Brad was coming?"

"I didn't invite him." She pulled another Taittinger bottle from the fridge. "Susie, I would never."

"Why didn't you tell me about dinner? You're such great pals, Brad can just stroll into your party?"

"Please tell me you're not into Brad again." She uncorked the bottle.

"No. Of course not." I wiped the overflow with a towel. "I'm married."

"Don't rub it in," she said, drinking from the bottle. "Did I tell you that Hans said he was converting to Judaism and getting circumcised? Now that he's gone. Does that mean he wants to come back? Or that he wants to be the perfect Jewish man to spite me?"

"Maybe he'll cut off the tip and send it to you," I offered.

"Could be Hitler guilt," she mused. "Where's your wedding ring?"

"Getting it cleaned. Please don't like Paul again."

"Didn't we have this conversation fifteen years ago?"

"Eighteen." I shook my head, lit another smoke. She took a drag, though she'd quit too. I flashed to a dorm party sophomore year. Claire and I were sitting on the floor of the bathroom getting stoned, making a blood pact that we'd never speak to Brad or Paul again.

She went for the doorbell one more time.

When I peeked out, I caught Brad switching business cards with Dirk. Dirk never gave me an assignment; I'd kill him if Brad wound up writing for *Vanity Fair*. Animal copulation, the hot new subject.

I thought of parties in Ann Arbor, where Brad and I came separately but left together. He'd catch my eye from across the room, signal toward the door. Most of the time I only showed up in order to go home with him. He would rip off my clothes the second we walked into his apartment and throw me to the floor. Did I still want to go home with him?

Brad kissed my cheek and said, "I have to go."

Before I could figure out a retort, he was gone. I plopped down on the couch, ate pâté, and tried to recover. I knew everyone here. It was my scene, my city. So what if I didn't look gorgeous tonight? I was tall and popular. Trauma averted. Paul sat down next to me.

"Brad had a dinner meeting," he explained. "I'm glad everyone's friends again."

"Just like college." I ate crackers and cheddar cheese and olives; I hadn't eaten all day.

"He gave me a copy of the Howard Stern tape. Want to see it?"

I shook my head no, tried the Brie on a Triscuit.

"You told me to marry Claire ten years ago," Paul went on. "You were right."

"Where's her ring?" I asked him.

"Where's your ring?" He lifted my hand.

"At the jeweler's, adding a stone," I mumbled, Triscuits in my mouth. Why was everyone guarding my ring? In this crowd I was the only one married—they needed me to be married. Or did I need them not to be?

"I like Claire. We're having fun."

"It's not about fun," I said. It was about marriage; how dumb was he? I glanced at his watch: 1 A.M. How could it be 1 A.M.? I just got here. Aaron was on the plane, halfway home, nine more hours. I had to hurry home to wait for him. I went for my coat. Paul followed.

"Want to see my place? It's not very far from here." He helped me get my hands into the holes.

"Going home," I said. I found Claire, flirting with Gary. A miracle—she made it out of the kitchen to talk to the already circumcised guy, a comedy writer, like Aaron. Good, I'd forgotten that's why I'd invited him. "I love you," I told her.

She put her arm around Gary and said, "I love my present," and winked. "Can you get home okay? The doorman can get you a cab."

"I'll put her in one," Paul offered, kissing Claire on the lips. "I'll call you later."

"Call her tomorrow," I butted in, glad he was going so she could sleep with Gary.

Outside, Paul flagged me down a taxi. I got in. "Thanks," I said but Paul jumped in next to me. "Seventy-fifth and Fifth," he told the driver.

"Eighth and Broadway," I said. Why had I eaten that pâté? I hated pâté. "I forgot my umbrella."

"You've never seen my place," Paul said.

"It's one o'clock in the morning. No house tours. Where's my umbrella?"

"I'll buy you a new one. Just for a minute. Please," he begged.

"You're kidnapping me?" I was incredulous for a second, then amused. I hadn't been on a drunk New York adventure in years. Aaron never drank; we never went north of Fourteenth Street. This was almost fun. We stopped at Paul's fancy building, which looked like Claire's fancy building. My single friends had all become rich. When did that happen? Paul led me through his lobby, into the elevator. I brushed my hair in the mirror on the ceiling.

"Wait till you see the marble. They just finished." He reached for the key. Inside, the lights were on. Brad was sitting on the living room couch, watching TV.

"Thought you had a dinner," Paul said.

"They didn't show." Brad shrugged. "I ordered Chinese. Hi Sue. Want some chicken and broccoli?"

Okay, what the heck was going on here? I hadn't seen Brad in ten years, now he was everywhere. I was stuck in the Twilight Zone, the one with the hideously ugly girl who couldn't get home to her planet, where she was beautiful.

"You told him to marry Claire ten years ago," Brad said.

I should have known Brad would be staying at Paul's. They'd been best friends since high school. I couldn't have not known. I didn't know. I had to have known.

"She was right," Paul said, sitting down on the couch next to Brad. I sat on the other side. They put on the video of Brad on Howard Stern, talking about the male black widow spider, who breaks off his penis inside the female spider, preventing her from ever mating again. When the act is completed, the female kills and eats the male. Out of all the sex stories in the animal kingdom, it was funny that Brad had chosen that one. The ultimate male fear: if you loan us your penis, we'll keep it. Then we'll kill you.

"Doesn't he look great?" Paul asked.

"He looks great," I said. Had Paul set me up? I looked at him, chipper and happy, having his two oldest friends over to his new place. He'd always looked up to me and Brad. Paul was on a different spaceship altogether, desperate to re-create college and reunite his fantasy parents. He bounced to the kitchen.

"Everything okay?" Brad looked at me. "You seem upset."

"Did you not answer my last e-mail for three weeks 'cause you're scared?" I blurted.

Brad nodded.

"To feel close to me?"

"Yes."

That was the problem with honesty, it didn't end. You always needed to keep going further.

"Can I give you a tour?" Paul offered, in the nick of time.

"Sure," I said, then followed him through his new sparsely furnished eight rooms. He pointed to working fireplaces, Italian marble, original moldings. He was empty inside too, I gathered, filling the void with blank spaces. I said it was lovely. Back in the living room, Brad was watching himself on TV again; now there were two of him. I yelled, "See you later" and ran out of there fast.

*   *   *

No matter what time I went to bed drunk I always opened my eyes at 6 A.M.—God's revenge. Even if I took aspirin. Thus the next morning at six o'clock, the day of Aaron's arrival, I woke up sick to my stomach. The waiting for Aaron wasn't even over—there were four more hours. I cleaned the apartment, did laundry. The phone rang at 7:45, when I was folding towels. Nobody ever called so early. I thought it must be Aaron from the airport.

"Hey. How are you feeling?" asked Brad.

"Where are you?"

"At the airport. Are you okay?"

"Why were you crawling around Claire's party?" It was too early to monitor myself. "Go back to Boston and marry your twenty-four-year-old."

"You were pretty out of it." He laughed. "Did you open your eyes at 5 A.M.?"

"Six," I said. "Stop knowing everything about me! Claire is off-limits! Don't talk to her. She's mine! Unless Paul marries her."

"I hope she slept with Gary. Did you know we all have the same decorator?"

"You have an interior decorator?" That was the last straw. "Who the hell are you? First a book, now you're a freelancer with a decorator?"

"You told me all about your infertility last night," he said.

"I did not." I hadn't said more than two words to him. "Forget everything I said." Why was I whispering? Airports, secrets. The call felt illicit. With Brad, I used to think the hot sex justified the headaches. Now all I had were the headaches. What was the point of that?

"I'll be back in New York next week," he said.

"Let's not do lunch." I had to hang up. I couldn't talk to Brad, Aaron was coming.

"You'll be happy to know my book got killed in the *Times Book*

Review," he slipped in. "Next week's; my editor got an advance copy."

"It doesn't make me happy. You have no idea what makes me happy." I wished it did make me happy, but I felt bad knowing how lousy he felt. I could read his silence, he was devastated. "I'm sorry. Some of those *Book Review* critics are frustrated they can't publish their own books so they trash everyone else's."

"You write for them," he said.

"Case closed." No wonder he had been quiet last night. I'll bet he didn't have dinner plans; he just snuck out of the party so he wouldn't have to tell me. It was easier now, on his way out of town. I felt like crying, about his review, about admitting that Aaron and I couldn't have a baby.

"But you're always respectful. You won't kill anyone," he said.

"Every journalist is a murderer," I said.

I thought of surprising Aaron at the door, wearing the four-inch-high sandals with my black silk nightgown; I'd had it cleaned. But I felt too queasy to change out of my baggy jeans. And my feet hurt from wearing high-heeled boots to Claire's. Aaron trudged in at ten o'clock, rumpled and tired, bearing presents. A Barbie doll in a Korean wedding dress. A silver bracelet and a purple pashmina like the one I'd just bought for Claire. That was odd. "You got me a purple one last year," I shouldn't have said.

"I did? Not black?" He was crushed.

"I love the Barbie Dools. Is that how they say doll in Korean?"

"Probably a typo," he said.

"It's pretty. I finished my *Times* review. I printed it out. And I took some messages for you." I ran to get the yellow Post-it note I'd stuck on my calendar. When I lifted it off I noticed I'd starred this weekend: it was my ovulation window. I handed Aaron the pages and numbers, kissed his neck, and hugged him. He felt good. "Want to fool around?"

"Too tired," Aaron said. "Couldn't sleep on the plane."

"It's a good time," I said, using our code for the day I was ovulating, rubbing his shoulders.

"I'll read it tomorrow." He dropped my piece on the table. He didn't remember.

I was about to explain that if we hurried we could catch the end of my forty-eight-hour cycle—incredible timing. Then it hit me. It didn't matter anymore. The fertility doctors had confirmed we couldn't get pregnant.

"But I haven't seen you in three weeks." I was clinging, still wanting him.

"I've gotta crash for a few hours." He squirmed out of my grip.

"I will too. I couldn't sleep last night," I said, leaving out the rest.

I had a cigarette in the living room, reread the review. My mistake wasn't asinine. Even if the author had died three years later, memory still could have killed him.

In the bedroom it looked like a monsoon had hit, my big messy man back again. Clothes were all over the room, sneakers in the middle of the floor—I almost tripped on them. The window was wide open even though it was forty degrees; he was already hogging the white down quilt, wrapped around him like a cocoon. It was freezing. I hoped to seduce him but he was out cold, didn't even stir when I sneaked in. Though we usually slept on our own sides of the bed, without touching, tonight I slipped my hands under his T-shirt, palms against his back. His skin was warm. I put my feet under his calves and pressed against him while he snored, using his body as a heater.

8

I called Richard Lacks," I told my mother over the phone. "I found him in Westchester. I left a message."

"Why would he call you back?" she asked.

"If an ex called you after fifteen years, wouldn't you have a cup of coffee?" I said. "Just out of curiosity?"

"No," she said. "I'd be afraid they'd bring a gun."

My mother had a point. Richard had reason to fear me. Our year and a half had ended in a melodramatic war involving dueling exes, angry magazine editors, a dog with three mothers, and a loony, cat-loving landlord; it was my own personal Vietnam.

This was probably why I loved reading gossip about famous people's big messy public breakups. No matter how rich or talented or smart you were, sex gone wrong could turn your life into an ugly circus. It made me feel better knowing this transcended race, class, and geography. Bad love was universal—the great leveler.

Love gone right was quieter. I hadn't heard much about Richard in recent years. Just that he was married, had a daughter, and wrote books in a ritzy suburb nearby. I left a message for him on Sunday afternoon. By Sunday night I regretted it. Leaving a message for a guy always made me jittery. I had to wait and see if it would be returned or ignored. When I was single I'd never leave a guy I liked a phone message. I'd call a hundred times, hanging up if he didn't answer. (Luckily this was before caller ID.) Liberated or not, you were still better off when a guy called you—even after you were married.

Richard had first called when I was twenty-four, an editorial assistant at *The New Yorker*. He was a divorced freelance journalist working on a biography of Bob Dylan. Knowing I was a Dylan fanatic, a friend gave him my number. He invited me for a home-cooked dinner. No straight guy had offered to cook me dinner before (or since). I was impressed.

I'd walked to his West Village brownstone that early summer evening, July Fourth weekend. I was worried that I might look overeager in my low-cut sleeveless knit sweater and short black skirt. A tall, forty-four-year-old guy, with pepper-and-salt hair to his shoulders, opened the door. He looked a little like Dylan, in black jeans and a gray silk shirt, silver earring dangling from his left lobe. He was sexy. My mother would hate him.

"Susan. Hi. Right on time," he said. "Come on in."

"Thanks." I regretted not being late.

He led me through a long hallway into his living room. I was in awe—it was the nicest Village apartment I'd ever seen, with exposed brick walls and original moldings at the edges of the high ceilings. The built-in shelves, which must have been seven feet high, were neatly stacked with thick books. I spotted Victor Navasky and Bob Woodward; he was mostly nonfiction, all hardcover.

"Someone else will be joining us tonight," he told me. "I hope you don't mind."

I immediately feared a weird sexual triangle, but when Richard opened a side door, a medium-sized mutt with white and brown fur bounded out, jumping and barking. I hated dogs.

"This is Oscar," he said. "He wants you to pet him."

Oscar sidled up to me, stuck his face in my hand, and licked me. The dog was going to be a problem. I pulled away and he barked. "Oscar likes you." Richard looked me up and down. "He's got a thing for gorgeous brunettes."

By the time he finished giving me a tour of his elegant railroad flat, I was falling for him. It ended in the dining room, which had lace curtains and a French country table set for two in the corner, his own Parisian bistro. Nice seduction method—feed 'em and fuck 'em. I might have been from Michigan, but I was an old twenty-four.

"Tell me about your book," I said, sitting down.

"Tell me about your work," Richard countered. "I checked out some back issues of *Cosmo*." He uncorked a bottle of red wine. "I loved your friend who just met the man she wanted to father the children she didn't want to have."

My first national publication; he'd done his research. He poured a little wine into a fancy fluted crystal glass. Then he handed it to me to taste, an act wasted on a diet soda doyenne, but I went along, nodding.

"You've done five 'Outrageous Opinions' in a row. Funniest stuff in the magazine," he said.

Uh-oh. He read all five. That meant he knew about my therapy with Dr. G., my redheaded mother who sent pink angora sweaters that shed, and the gory details of my last three psychotic breakups. Nothing like being mysterious. I drank up while he brought out salad with four shades of lettuce in a ceramic bowl. Oscar followed, then sat at Richard's feet. Good, I didn't want the dog near me.

"You should try my editor at *Vogue*. Leon Booth. Use my name, Susan."

"Everyone calls me Sue." I made a mental note of Booth's name. I'd heard that *Vogue* paid two dollars a word.

"I'd rather call you Susan," he said.

"What have you done for *Vogue*?" I asked.

"A bunch of celebrity interviews." He poured dressing on the salad. "Madonna, Bruce, and Mick."

Worse than name-dropping was first-name dropping. I wondered if he really knew all those famous musicians. I pointed to the series of framed Billy Joel records on the wall. "What are those?"

"Everything Billy touches turns to gold. I used to work with him. Booking, promo. I got tired of being on the road," he said. "I've also profiled politicians, actors, and businessmen."

There was a door off the kitchen. To the bedroom. That was convenient, though I preferred sex on an empty stomach. I felt warm from the wine. I hadn't eaten all day, just in case. I'd never slept with a guy on a first date before.

"You're from Michigan. I just pitched a piece out there. Lee Iacocca." He finished off the bottle, opened another.

"My dad knows him through a close friend at Chrysler," I said. I tried the salad—the dressing was too tangy.

"*Life* magazine said they'd give me a cover. But so far Iacocca hasn't agreed."

"Let me know if you have trouble," I offered. "I might be able to help you with that one."

He cleared the table, returning with bowls of flute-shaped pasta and salmon. I hated salmon. He held a copy of *Playboy* magazine under his arm and opened it to a picture of himself with Billy Joel. Underneath it read: "Journalist Richard Lacks worked in the music biz for fifteen years." He looked cute in the photo, but it was still a skin rag. I expected him to leave it open to naked bunnies at a car wash. But he put it away and refilled my glass. If he was trying to get me drunk it was working.

"Tell me about your book," I said again.

"Let's see." He ran his fingers through his hair. I wanted to run my fingers through it. "We signed a six-figure deal with Simon & Schuster. My agent's got the biggest balls in the business."

I wanted to hear about the intricacies of the lyrics, not the deal.

"An old boyfriend used to send me words to Dylan's love songs," I said. "All tortured. I should have taken the hint."

"His songs don't even touch the surface."

"Tell, tell," I said, as the dog slipped over to my side. I petted him and he wagged his tail. At least Oscar was easy.

"He makes up stories. You know his famous motorcycle accident?"

I nodded, of course I knew, I had been obsessed with Dylan since I was fifteen.

"I'm not so sure there really was a motorcycle accident," Richard said.

"Really?" I didn't believe it. "Tell me more." I took out a cigarette. He lit it. When he went to the kitchen I picked out the salmon from my bowl and fed it to Oscar. Richard came out with an ashtray, a chunk of cheese, and a grater. He scraped cheese on my pasta, then on his.

"He drove his first girlfriend mad."

"The one on the album cover?"

He inched closer, took a cigarette from my pack, and lit it ineptly, like someone who only smoked at parties. My hands were sweating.

"She was young. He seduced her, but he was also sleeping with other women." He put his arm around me and said, "When she found out the truth she tried to kill herself. Her name was Susie."

I put out my cigarette. Only my parents and Claire called me Susie. "How did you find out?"

"She told me," he said. "I can make people relax and tell me everything."

"Is that so?"

"Sometimes I think everyone's just waiting to spill their secrets."

"Writers are always selling someone out," I quoted Joan Didion.

"Two writers," he smirked. "That means our kids will be doctors."

I almost choked. He couldn't know I came from a family of doctors. My essay "The Disease Game" wouldn't be out in *Cosmo* until next month. Why did he think I wanted children?

"That was why my marriage didn't work. My wife decided she didn't want kids," he said. "I lived with another woman, Sally, for two years, but she couldn't have any."

The friend who had fixed us up wasn't sure if Richard was through with her. "When did you end it?"

"A few months ago," he said. "It was a bad breakup. Sally's a little crazy."

A lot of women were going crazy around here. I thought of my colleague Monica's warning: Listen carefully to what a man says about his exes, since you might soon be one of them. She'd also said, "Stay away from biographers. They leech on other people's lives." She had been single at the time and I thought she was jealous that I was going on a blind date with someone who sounded so successful.

"Do you want kids?" he asked.

I finished my wine. "I'd rather have books."

"Can't you have both, Susan?" He moved closer, stared into my eyes.

"Not before dessert," I said, feeling tipsy and gorgeous.

He smiled and went back to the kitchen for fresh raspberries and cream, which he served in two crystal glasses. They looked gorgeous too. Boy, this guy had a lot of crystal. He put on *Blood on the Tracks*. I waited for him to seduce me and dump me like Dylan did to that other Susie.

"Listen, I'm on deadline now," he said. "I hope you won't mind making it an early night."

"Not at all," I lied, looking at my watch. It was nine thirty. I felt rejected. The only guy I'd ever wanted to sleep with on a first date didn't want to sleep with me.

"I have to walk Oscar," he said. "Can we escort you home?" Or maybe he did.

"First tell me something juicy," I said. "What's Dylan like deep down? A genius or a drifter? Is he just insecure?"

"It's hard to figure out. He's created a mythology about his life. There's a lot of conflicting stories." Richard picked up a raspberry and fed it to me. Then he moved closer. "A real sociopath," he whispered in my ear.

9

Our first year was romantic. We sat on the stoop with Oscar, drinking wine and quoting Kakfa, as if we were important émigré writers in Paris. Richard critiqued every word I wrote. "Good. But tweak the last few lines," he'd say. "Twist the ending. Don't give me what I expect, surprise me."

He surprised me in bed, when he insisted I come first, refusing to climax if I didn't. When he did come, he called me gorgeous again. The flattery—and the chivalrous way he slept with his arm lightly around my waist—seemed a good argument for older men. I let him talk me into giving up my sublet and resigning from *The New Yorker* to be a freelancer, like him. (The argument against older men.)

We took Oscar on long walks through hidden parks in the Village, mingling with a subculture of urban dog nuts. I must have begun to smell like Oscar because, even when I was alone, local dogs came up to me. "Oh look Fifi, it's Oscar's mom!" Fifi's owner would say, waving.

Not long after I moved in, Richard's penchant for gourmet cooking, so lovely and nurturing on our first date, became a tedious headache. He was horrified that I preferred diet soda to wine and iceberg lettuce to romaine. "You have the most unsophisticated palate in the country," he accused. He insisted that we go food shopping together and make elaborate dinners every night at six. His parents had divorced when he was young, and he found comfort in the domestic rites he'd missed. I, on the other hand, had overdosed on my family's sadistic dinner rituals. I delighted in skipping it, preferring junk food at midnight movies, or getting stoned and drinking diet sodas at seedy all-night diners Richard refused to set foot in.

There were other bad signs. He screwed up my phone messages. He paid bills late. His landlord and creditors left angry messages. Sally, his ex, began calling, screaming when I picked up the phone. Once we left the apartment to find tapes, letters, and presents he'd given her on fire on the stoop. "I told you she's wacko," he said. Quickly detaching the fire extinguisher from the wall, he put out the fire. Expertly. Had it happened before?

When Richard's father, a salesman from Pennsylvania, took us to dinner, he called me "Sally" all night. "My dad's passive-aggressive," Richard said. "Just ignore him." He never asked about his son's work and made callous jokes about Richard "getting a real job." No wonder Richard inflated his success. He had to bolster himself up, no one else in his life did. Of course he loved Dylan, a chameleon who shed his middle-class Jewish roots and reinvented himself as a rough-and-tumble troubadour.

Richard began traveling a lot, using Dylan research as an excuse for rambling around the country. I didn't mind that he was gone; I minded that he left the dog. I had a lifelong fear of dogs, ever since a neighbor's German shepherd had jumped and scratched me when I was three. My brothers always wanted a dog but I said, "I'm never living in the same house as a dog!" They voted to get one and get rid of me.

"Please. I can't put him in a kennel," Richard begged. "Oscar loves you. So do I."

I reluctantly agreed to try to get over my dog phobia by taking care of Oscar for a week. My fear was soon replaced by annoyance. The dog jumped on the bed at six o'clock every morning, and he needed to be fed and walked three times a day. It screwed up my schedule. I felt chained to the apartment. I hated cleaning up his dog doo on the street and pulling Oscar away from the male dogs he tried to pounce on. Richard had showed me how to break up a dogfight by stepping in the middle and pulling on the leash. If it got ugly, I planned to let go of the leash and run the other way.

Along with the miserable dog-parenting trial, a series of late-night phone hang-ups put me on edge. I sensed it was another woman calling. Claire said, "If something feels weird, it is." I scavenged through Richard's desk, confirming my suspicion: letters from another woman. Not Sally, who was at least a known quantity, but someone named Beth. In the middle of one letter, my eyes caught the sentence "I'm glad your friend Susan is making progress, but you're right, she sounds so young." It was dated September, two months after I had moved in. Your friend Susan?

That night Richard called from Michigan. He was going ahead with his profile of Lee Iacocca for *Life*. My father had set up the interview through his good friend at Chrysler. I confronted Richard long distance. "Who's Beth?"

"A friend," he said.

"The way I'm your friend?" I asked. "Like she said in that letter?"

"Are you going through my desk?" he yelled. "I can't handle this."

I slammed down the receiver. I'd done the sick love triangle with David in college. I was stuck in a revival of my worst oedipal nightmare. I had to get out. The next day I hired a local dog walker from Penny's Pooches to take Oscar. I scanned newspapers for sublets and found a loft share on West Twenty-sixth Street for six hundred dollars a month. I could almost afford it. I went to see the place and decided to take it. My part of the space, separated by a door, was a thousand square feet. The loft's owner, Donna, a disheveled woman in her fifties, was a former opera singer. I was a wreck. I told her that my live-in boyfriend was seeing someone else and I needed a place fast. She was sympathetic. For six hundred dollars cash, I could move in that day. Cats prowled the hallway, but at least there were no dogs. A friend with a van helped me throw everything I owned into garbage bags. I was unpacked in two hours.

At first Donna was sweet and motherly. She brought me chicken soup, helped me hang curtains, and told me about the cads in her past. But after Brad the boomerang spent the night consoling me, Donna changed her tune. Things started going wrong. Heat and electricity were turned off. Elevators stopped working. I found roaches and mice and had to wrap all food with aluminum foil and plastic bags. I couldn't find certain books, sweaters, and jewelry. Was Donna taking my stuff? It was disorienting, coming home each night to search for what else was gone.

Richard was not happy to get home and find me and Oscar missing. He somehow tracked down my phone number and left angry messages. He claimed I owed him money for the dog walker and phone bill and accused me of leaving him for another man and stealing his favorite Dylan T-shirts. Between rodents, Donna, and Richard, I was paranoid, afraid to come home or answer the phone. Claire bought me a card with a picture of a cute young girl in a red leotard and devil's horns that said "Gidget Goes to Hell."

One night a rustling noise woke me. On the counter I saw a huge rat gnawing through the aluminum foil and plastic wrap I had used to cover a bowl of popcorn. I called Claire at 4 A.M. She said, "You're moving in with me. Now."

This was embarrassing because, when Claire lived in Washington, I had begged her to move to New York, boasting about how marvelous Manhattan was and how I had an incredible boyfriend with an amazing pad. I swore we'd help her land a spacious place, job, and boyfriend too. A month after she moved to an alcove studio on

Horatio Street, I was crashing on her couch. "This is why I wanted you here," I said, hugging her at 5 A.M. that morning. "To save my life."

The next day my father called me at Claire's. It seemed that Lee Iacocca had tied the knot to his second wife, and *Life* magazine had exclusive photos. Richard's editor toned down Richard's provocative political piece on Iacocca in favor of a nicer piece with a big wedding spread. Richard then sold the controversial outtakes of his Iacocca interview to *Newlook*, a *Penthouse* spin-off. My father, his friend, Iacocca, and Chrysler's attorney were not happy. This was a new one, an ex not only screwing me over, but screwing over my relatives and family friends. In West Bloomfield, my breakup stories were becoming legendary.

Three months after I left Richard I learned that his new size three was a quiet, rich art director he was marrying. Marrying!!! I couldn't eat or sleep, blaming myself. I was too big, loud, and poor—he had met someone better. I crawled to the Village Den around the corner to read the *Times* and cry into my diet Pepsi. I saw Sally, Richard's ex ex. I recognized her from pictures in the desk drawer I wasn't supposed to ransack. She was prettier in person. Lonely, broke, and lost in self-pity, I mumbled, "You don't have to hate me anymore. Richard and I split up."

"You poor thing. It's not your fault." Sally slid into my booth and took my hand. "These things are so horrible." She was a little WASPy redhead, Richard's age. I expected her to be crazy, but she seemed wise, warm, empathetic. She wasn't the one who was crazy. *He* was crazy! "I bet he was seeing someone else, lying to you. That's what he does." Sally handed me a Kleenex. "He's a sociopath. So is his father. Whenever that man came to town he called me Connie, Richard's ex-wife."

"He called me Sally," I said, and she cracked up. "Richard is seeing someone else. Beth." I blew my nose. "They're getting married."

Sally was more shocked than I was. I should have realized that this was strange—they had split more than two years before. But I liked her spin better. I wasn't to blame—Richard was, or his father, or the Lacks's family legacy. "You're only guilty of believing what someone you love told you," Sally said and I nodded enthusiastically.

An actress-turned-writer, Sally read my work and hooked me up with editors, taking over where Richard had left off. I didn't need a lover, I needed a manager. She showed me photos of her, Richard, and Oscar, whom they had bought together. She couldn't get over the fact that Richard took the dog. "I thought we were getting married. Then he says he's on deadline for the week and I see him walking with a woman—twenty years younger than I am—with my dog." Sally's rage made sense to me—she couldn't have a child. Oscar was the baby in their rendition of *Who's Afraid of Virginia Woolf?*

At parties Sally pointed out people who hated Richard, her world divided into Richard's friends and Richard's foes. My Richard addiction was waning as I fell for Brad and his mammoth shoulders again. "Out of the frying pan . . ." I told Claire. "You're allowed to use a bad ex to get you over a worse ex," Claire assured me. She just wanted me out of her living room. She found another studio available in her building, which I sublet.

One August afternoon a few months later, Sally and I were strolling down Bleecker Street. I was telling her about a *New York Times* editor who liked my work, when we saw Richard. He turned the corner with the dog, a petite dark-haired woman by his side. He saw us and stopped cold, his mouth open. He handed the dog's leash to his companion, obviously the fiancée. He didn't know that Sally and I were pals. He was stunned. "Susan. Sally," he said. Finally face-to-face with her long-term tormentor, Sally gasped and flailed her arms, like she was having a seizure.

Oscar twisted around, getting tangled in the leash, barking his head off. Richard grabbed the leash and said, "Down, boy, down." Oscar went bonkers anyway. He freed himself and made a beeline for me and Sally, who bent down and kissed him gleefully. I petted him too; I'd actually missed the mutt. He slobbered all over us, jumping and squealing. He'd found his two long-lost mommies!

"Hi Richard," I said.

"Susan. Sally. Susan. Sally," he kept saying, like the scene in *Chinatown*.

I had never considered myself impressionable. Yet Dr. G. said being around crazy people was a quick way to be crazy. I admit that that spring, with Sally's input (and lighter fluid), I had burned the stuff Richard had given me on his stoop. I'd started calling him by Sally's nickname, "The Sociopath," and matched his mean phone messages, blustering, "Oh yeah, well I heard Iacocca's lawyer wants to sue you. . . . And I'm telling Dylan's publicist all the bullshit you're spreading, so they'll probably sue you too!" This ended when Richard moved away. His Dylan book came out around the same time as three other Dylan biographies, none of which caught on. It took a few hundred therapy sessions to unravel the mess.

Now that I was about the age Richard had been when we met, another side of the story surfaced. Looking over my twenty-year career, I realized he had been pivotal. Because of him I left a clerical job to go out on my own. He said freelancers like him made a hundred thousand dollars a year, and it was a fantastic way to make a living that I could easily pull off. I believed him. Luckily I didn't figure out that he was delusional until years later. You needed to be a bit sociopathic to be a freelance writer. His visions of grandeur freed me.

When Aaron came home that night, I told him that I'd called

Richard, and shared my new take on Richard's purpose in my life. "He had everything I wanted—a warm Village apartment, magazine work, a big book contract."

"You didn't want to date him, you wanted to be him," Aaron said.

"Yes! And I am him. But not the him he really was, the him I wanted him to be." I was thrilled with my revisionist history, which made me look less stupid, the most painful year of my life twisted into a clever career strategy. Another benefit of aging.

"I'm going to sleep," Aaron said, less enamored of my theory than I was. "I'm exhausted."

On Monday I found a message from Richard. I was glad he hadn't erased me like an insignificant footnote. Then again, he was a biographer, an investigative journalist, a snoop. He was curious why I'd called after fifteen years. Every story had an addendum. I tried him again. This time he answered the phone. "Thanks for calling me back," I said. "Are you surprised to hear from me?"

"A little," he said.

"I'm turning forty, having a midlife crisis, writing about all the stupid things I did in my past . . ." I turned the meeting into work, as I'd done with Brad; work was safer.

"You weren't stupid," Richard cut me off. He said it in a kind voice. An older voice, like the mentor he'd been when we went out.

"Our breakup was horrible. I was ridiculous." I was being self-deprecatingly honest and manipulative at the same time. I wanted a cathartic revelation, but also a favor. He was number four on my list. I wanted to see him. Tomorrow.

"You were hurt," he said.

From this angle, it was mundane. I was once in love with him. It didn't work out, so he wed someone else. I had overlapped many times myself. It was hard to avoid, since one was most attractive when one was sexually unavailable. The same way that it was easier to find a job when you already had one.

"You were never stupid," he repeated, as if he knew it was my worst fear, that a man would think I wasn't smart. His words somehow erased the ugliness lodged somewhere in my soul all these years and I felt younger. On the verge of a breakthrough. The man who I feared didn't think I was smart enough was my father. That might be why I had the idea to see my exes now. Before I became a mother, I needed absolution from all my father figures.

"I was wondering . . . if you're ever in the city . . . could we have a cup of coffee, or lunch?" I asked. A place to confess? "I'll meet you anywhere you want . . ."

"Can we go somewhere with metal detectors?" he asked.

"That's just what my mother said," I laughed, thankful that it finally seemed funny.

1 O

Richard and I made a lunch plan for noon on Wednesday. The night before I was giddy. Meeting old lovers was exciting; I highly recommend all happily married people do it. There's a buzz, like first-date jitters, or going to your high school reunion, but better. You get an hour of undivided attention from the person you most want to talk to, the one you slept with, who had an old picture of you in a drawer he'd pull out if you asked. I was asking. With no serious threat of sex, there was no anxiety.

Or so I thought. After telling Aaron to wake me up at ten on Wednesday (I was always a late riser), I couldn't sleep. I finally shut my eyes at 7 A.M. and opened them at 11:15. My husband, usually more reliable than my alarm clock, had left without waking me— he'd forgotten. Let's analyze that one. I looked in the mirror. Just what I needed—bags under my eyes so I'd look even older to my ex. I jumped in the shower and threw on safety clothes: black jeans and black sweater.

Before I ran out, I went to the closet and carefully removed two old T-shirts from the top shelf: "Hibbing, Minnesota" and "The Newport Jazz Festival." I'd found them when we moved five years ago. I must have inadvertently thrown them into a garbage bag fifteen years before and never noticed. Accidents were too easy—I had stolen Richard's stuff. I'd lied to both of us.

I hopped the subway to the Upper West Side cafe he'd chosen. Worried about being late, I was ten minutes early. I sat in a booth in the back and did the *Times* crossword puzzle in pen. I told myself if I finished the whole puzzle without mistakes, he'd appear. If I left any blank, he wouldn't show. Halfway through I looked up and saw Richard walking in. He waved and walked toward me. He had short hair, all white. He was in a dark suit. We shook hands and he sat down. Same face but the short, white hair threw everything off.

"The hair," I said. I couldn't help staring.

"I know. I cut it seven years ago."

"I've been dyeing mine for seven years," I offered.

"Ten," he said. "You wrote a 'Hers' column about it. 'Fear of Dyeing.'"

The boy still did his homework. "You look good, just really . . ."

"I know," he cut me off. "Mr. Suburbs."

"I can't believe you left the city." I noted he didn't say a thing about my looks; was I a total disappointment? Maybe it wasn't appropriate.

"I can't believe I left the city," he said. "It's death, but the schools are better for my daughter."

He was clean cut, older, normal-seeming and nice, but a totally different guy I never would have fallen for. I liked the self-deprecation about the burbs and the mention of his daughter.

"I hear you're writing a book on the Rolling Stones," I said.

"My editor at Random House got me a huge advance," he said. "He's their top guy. My agent already sold it to the movies. I'm doing the script. I was just in Paris, talking to Mick about it."

"Nobody ever changes," Aaron the cynic always said. From this vantage point Richard's name-dropping didn't bug me. He didn't really lie—70 percent of what he said was true. He just puffed everything up a bit, made himself more important. There was something almost poignant about it.

"I read about your wedding in the *Times*," he said. "How'd you meet Aaron?"

"A friend fixed us up," I said. "Aaron was working on *Saturday Night Live*. I fell in love, then two weeks later he took a job on *Seinfeld* in L.A. I thought it was over, but he sent me a plane ticket for the weekend. I stayed two months." I was name-dropping too, trying to impress him back. We had the same issue, after all: desperately wanting our fathers' attention and approval. I'd spent hours dissecting it with Dr. G.

"Your grandfather was emotionally abusive," she'd once said. "Your father wasn't."

"He seemed neglectful when I was growing up. Like he was never really there."

"Your father was always there. He loved you. It was just easier for him to communicate with your brothers," she said. "Usually someone abused repeats the pattern. Your father didn't, he changed."

Though Aaron didn't think people changed, Dr. G. said there were three ways they could: through therapy, the death of a parent, or healthy love. My mother had saved my father. Richard's father left his mother—that was what wrecked him.

In some ways, Richard had been a paternal figure to me. He'd taught me to be confident, to promote myself. When someone asked who I wrote for I said "*The New York Times* and *Washington Post*." I had written for both. But not as often as my answer implied. The second lie was that he was the star fucker. I was too; I was his protégé.

Richard ordered wine, I ordered diet soda. I didn't want us to spend an hour showing off and one-upping each other, so I threw him a bone, so to speak.

"I have a story for you," I said. "About Sally."

"Are you still friends with her?" His expression changed.

"No, I haven't seen her in five years. She was so happy for me, I invited her to my wedding. After the ceremony I saw her regaling a group of my friends and relatives with a loud discourse about Richard Lacks. Sally was telling the whole saga, with different voices, dog barks, and hand gestures. Twenty years after you guys split. I thought, Okay, maybe she is kind of dotty."

He nodded but he wasn't laughing. "She threatened my daughter three months ago. I have an order of protection out against her," he said.

"Jesus." I didn't think Sally was capable of hurting anyone, but their ongoing animosity fascinated me. Richard and Sally had only dated for a few years two decades before; their hate was longer and more passionate than their love.

"That reminds me." He pulled a tiny tape recorder from his pocket and turned it on. For fellow journalists, it was like pulling out a gun. I hadn't brought mine. "I need to do one thing," he said. "Whatever you write, do you promise not to use my real name, my daughter's name, or the city where we live?"

"I do," I said into the machine. I thought he was going to record our entire talk, but he turned the recorder off and put it away. "It's nice that you're protecting your daughter."

"I'd die for her," he said with characteristic extremity, though it made me like him more.

He ordered linguine with mushrooms and peppers; I chose chicken.

"My palate's still unsophisticated," I said. "In *Diner*, the guy makes his fiancée take a sports test. Aaron made me do a food test—I had to eat Indian, Japanese, Thai, Malaysian, Burmese, and Brazilian before he'd marry me."

"You had chicken at every one," he said. "I read your piece, in *The Forward*."

"You read *The Forward*?"

That piece had been published in 1995. I suddenly saw my mother's side of our long-term fight about why I should muzzle myself, at least in print. After each piece she left messages. "Go ahead, tell the world you had a miserable childhood and it was all my fault." She'd taken to saying, "This is off the record," when I asked anything about the family.

"It's on-line," he said. He was an intellectual stalker. I was half-complimented, half-worried. What else had I given away? "Tell me about your book deal."

"My book deal?" I asked.

"You said you were writing about your past."

"I don't have a book deal," I admitted, flattered that he had elevated my heartbreak journey idea to book level. I'd been thinking more along the lines of a woman's magazine article.

"You'll definitely get a book," he said, like he had no doubt. The guy did listen and take me seriously. Just the strong way he talked about it made me think it was going to happen. I remembered how he used to call me Susan instead of Sue; Susan was more serious. "Did you see that guy from Canada? David?"

I was startled. David was from college, way before Richard. "Not yet," I said. Oh no, what had I I published about David?

"You used to talk about him a lot, the triangle. You weren't over him."

I didn't recall sharing my previous forays into triangulation.

"Is there anything specific you wanted to ask me?" he ventured.

"How old are you?" If he could take out a tape recorder, I could take out a notebook, which I did, along with a pen.

"I'm fifty-one," he said.

"Fifty-one? How old were you when we met?" I asked.

"I was thirty-six."

Lie number three—mine. I had aged him. It was more dramatic if he was twenty years my senior, more sordid—he could have really been my father. I was shocked that he was only eleven years older, the same age as Aaron. While eating and chatting, I investigated other details of Richard's life, to see what else my defenses had distorted. His wife was indeed Beth, but they wed three years after our demise. I was sure it had been three months; I'd upped the ante so I looked more victimized. I was awed by my fickle recollections, how I'd soothed myself with self-deception.

"How's Oscar?" I asked.

"He died four years ago. Don't get me started or I'll cry," Richard said. I never doubted that he adored the dog. "We have two more now. They look just like him."

"You and I were too different," I said. Beth was an early morning riser who liked dogs and cooking and travel, I gathered. Were we all looking for our clones? "Is that what you thought?"

"Well, to tell the truth . . ."

Aaron said *to tell the truth* was a dumb expression because it implied at all other times you weren't.

"When I met you I was just getting over my wife and Sally. In both relationships I was supporting them, financially and emotionally. I didn't want to be a caretaker anymore."

I felt a tinge of anger. I had been broke because he convinced me to be a freelancer. Man turns woman into someone he can't be attracted to.

"Beth owned her own apartment, business, and car. I was impressed. She cooked and took care of me . . ."

Ouch. I recalled hearing that Beth was successful, and that he'd moved into her place. She took care of Richard, the way I couldn't. It hurt to think of myself as unnurturing. Yet even now I had no desire to take care of a man, child, and pets in a big house in the suburbs, or to be taken care of. Aaron and I were independent, separate people. We basically took care of ourselves.

Richard talked about other books he'd published that I'd never heard of, a visiting professorship at Yale, where he taught a class in biography, jaunts to Paris, where they might move, his daughter who skied so well she might wind up on the Olympic ski team.

"Part of the motivation for what I'm writing is infertility," I admitted inanely, finding a way to get even more naked.

"How long have you been trying?" he asked.

"More than a year."

"We tried for four years," he said.

"Really? Four years?" One benefit to self-exposure, it was contagious.

"We didn't use doctors or specialists," he said. "A friend told us that after sex Beth should hold her legs in the air for an hour. That worked."

"I've heard that," I said, once again amazed at how infertility made everyone reveal intimate details of their sex life, like I did in print.

"When you have a baby, you'll understand my fear of Sally," he said.

I liked that he said "When you have a baby," the same way he kept saying "When your book comes out." The ludicrous overconfidence extended to everyone at his table.

"Thanks for meeting me," I said. "It's very cathartic. For you too?"

"Not really. I never had bad feelings about you. I liked seeing your work, I was proud of you," he said. "You know, I never lied to you. I told you things weren't working out before I started seeing Beth. I want you to know that."

It was more interesting that he wanted me to know, than whether or not it was true. It might have been true. After I moved in, we did argue a lot. He said things like, "This isn't working out," and, "Maybe we need a break." I hadn't been listening.

"Please stop writing that I lied to you about everything."

"I never wrote that," I said, honestly.

"You did," he said. "In *New Woman*."

"You read *New Woman*?"

"You can get anything on-line," he explained. This had to be cathartic for him; he'd been tracking my work for years. Or did he get it all in one search and memorize it yesterday? I published two pieces in *New Woman*. One was about a female boss I admired, the other was about the benefits of therapy. Richard was clearly wrong, but I didn't say so.

He insisted on treating me to lunch. I handed him the T-shirts I'd brought. He said he didn't remember them, but it felt good, giving him something back. It was nice that he'd made time to see me. At the curb I awkwardly hugged him good-bye. Walking home, I stopped at Victoria's Secret, where I charged five expensive push-up bras. One for each ex. Most men wanted a bigger penis. I wanted bigger breasts. To pump myself up?

At home I looked through my old issues of *New Woman*. I reread the essay about my boss—no mention of Richard. Then I scanned the second piece, about therapy. Toward the end I'd started a sentence: "At one point I was depressed when the man I lived with turned out to be a compulsive liar . . ."

Another self-lie. He was right. "Compulsive liar" was a slur. In the original draft, I recalled, I'd called him a "sociopath." I'd only toned it down when my editor said, "It won't play in Peoria." It was funny, I remembered my exes' compliments. They recalled my insults. That was why he'd wanted to meet—to ensure I wouldn't write anything else bad about him. I suddenly understood why all my exes found sweet, quiet mates—I'd chosen one myself.

"You forgot to wake me this morning for lunch with Richard," I told Aaron that night.

"Protecting you subconsciously," he said. "Did I need to?"

"No, lunch was nice." I brought a blanket into the Bat Cave; it was always freezing in there. "I saw why I liked him and why I married you."

"He published a bunch of books." Aaron sat next to me on the couch. "Six. I looked him up on the Net. Maybe you'd rather be with someone who writes books."

"He wants to write for the screen, like you do." The Net brought out the stalker in all of us. "And he said he's a professor at Yale. Teaching biography."

"I was offered a visiting professorship at NYU," Aaron said. "I forgot to tell you."

"Are you serious? That's great! When?" I asked, jealous. I'd been a lowly adjunct in their journalism school for years. I'd talked Aaron into teaching one NYU TV/film class last year.

"When did this happen?"

"Last week," he said.

"Why does everybody else get to be a professor when I'm the only one who loves to teach?"

"I wish you'd get a professorship," he said. "It's much easier in my program. It's hard to find good television teachers. No working TV writer with a brain would want to teach."

"That's not true," I argued. "I think it's impressive."

"Richard's a professor?" Aaron asked. "How many classes does he teach?"

"Two." Now I was lying to my husband. Richard had only mentioned one.

"You had a nice lunch?"

"Not that nice. He was upset about something mean I wrote about him years ago. I didn't even remember writing it."

"You hurt him too," Aaron said. "I taped *Law & Order*. Want to watch?"

"Sure. I think it's fantastic that you'll be a professor." I put my arm around him. "You okay?"

"Not feeling well. I almost fainted at the Writer's Guild meeting."

"Did you eat?" I asked.

"No," he said.

"What time was the meeting?"

"Three o'clock." He turned off the lights and rewound the tape. "And I didn't get any sleep last night."

That was odd, neither of us had slept or noticed each other awake. "Why the hell would you not eat anything until three?" I asked. "On no sleep yet."

In our marriage logic, I knew the answer. I was having lunch with my gourmet ex who'd hurt me. Aaron went on a food strike, voicing protest without realizing it. Ex number four, who didn't really unnerve me, unnerved my husband. I kissed Aaron and rubbed his neck, feeling guilty. But not guilty enough to give up my search for heartbreak number five.

11

November 2000
Root Canal

After unearthing the four most important men from my past, I was even more determined to locate my final heartbreak, who had actually been my first heartbreak. The Toronto operator said there were eight dentists listed under David Green. I left messages on all their office machines at midnight, hoping the David Green I had loved madly—from age fifteen to twenty—would call back. There was one problem: I forgot how polite Canadians were. For three days, it rained David Greens. All eight returned my call, none was him. They sounded nice. I felt bad, like I was disappointing them. Yet it was almost fun, as if rejecting eight David Greens could atone for the horrendous way my David Green had left me.

Love always paralyzed me, but work I could ace. To locate the lost David Green, I followed the trail leading back to my own dubious past. First I phoned my old friend Howard, who had been best friends with David in Herzl, the cutest male chapter of the B'nai B'rith teen group our parents made us all join.

"I meant to call David to tell him Jeff Katz died," Howard said. "But I don't have his number."

"Jeff Katz died?" He had been Herzl's treasurer. "Wasn't he our age?"

"Forty-one," Howard answered. "Heart attack. If you ever find David, tell him."

Sure. I'll surface out of nowhere, twenty-four years later, and open with, "Hey, David, how's it going, heard your old friend Jeff Katz just bit the dust." That would be endearing.

Then I recalled that David's kid brother, Kenny, had married Stacey Schwartz, a West Bloomfield girl. My mother knew her mother. I put my mother on the case, then called to check up.

"I haven't seen her," my mother said. "She's usually at the beauty shop on Saturdays, but she wasn't there this weekend."

"Look her up in the phone book."

"There are a thousand Schwartzes in West Bloomfield," she answered. "I can't remember her husband's name and didn't recognize the street address."

"Try harder."

"Now you're acting fifteen again," my mother snapped and hung up.

Finally I called my old Michigan pal Andrea, who knew Stacey from around the neighborhood. I begged her to get me David's anything: e-mail address, office phone number, or post office box. (I didn't want to call him at home and risk getting his wife.) Andrea, as always, came through, giving me his office e-mail. Yes!

On Monday night, with *Ally McBeal* in the background, I e-mailed David, typing "A voice from your past" in the subject box. "Hi. How are you?" I wrote. "I was hoping we could talk for a few minutes." My message was returned, "host unknown."

I asked Andrea for Stacey's number and called her myself, using my trump card: I had been at her husband's bar mitzvah. She agreed to recheck David's e-mail address. At 10 P.M. the phone rang.

"What kind of trouble are you stirring up twenty-four years later?" David asked.

"David! Hi! Thanks for calling." I was elated, not the least bit nervous. "How are you? There are eight David Green dentists in Toronto. You're hard to find."

"I try to keep it that way," he said with a teasing lilt.

"You're a root canal specialist. The equivalent of what you did to me emotionally." I'd slipped back into our old savage tone without meaning to.

"That's why I chose that specialty. To give you a good line." He sounded playful, amused to hear from me. "Now what the hell are you hounding my relatives for?"

"I'm writing an article about all the stupid things I did in my past . . ." The setup had worked wonders on Richard. I used it again, plagiarizing myself for a different audience.

"Is everything okay by you?" He sounded skeptical, as if there was another reason I was calling. Was there?

"Everything's great."

We caught up on friends (he had already heard Jeff Katz died) and family (he was married with an eleven-year-old son). He had also just watched *Ally McBeal* and said I reminded him of her. I found the character totally neurotic, but at least she was skinny. Did he remember me skinny? Or neurotic?

"How do you think of our past?" I asked. "I mean, if you ever think about it."

"I survived six years with Sue Shapiro. Thank God I got out of there alive."

"Really? No bad feelings?" I liked that he elevated it to six years. It had only been five.

"Really," he said. "It was a fun ride."

"You think fun ride. I think nuclear holocaust," I laughed. "No regrets at all?"

"I regret that I hurt your mother," he said. "I always loved that lady."

He refused to see me, but he gave me his correct e-mail (I'd transposed two letters) and told me to forward any questions. We'd been on the phone more than an hour, so I was glad it was on his bill. A root canal specialist could afford it; I'd paid enough. Right before we said good-bye, I threw out, "What's your wife like? What does she do?"

"Eve is smart, quiet. She's a housewife," he said.

"Petite?" I couldn't help but ask.

"Yeah, tiny," he said. "I bought her a dress last week, she's size two. Why do you ask?"

When we hung up, I dialed my mother, though it was 11:30 P.M. I usually didn't call after eleven. She was still up. I relayed the entire conversation.

"I loved him too," she remembered. "You were so intense, I was afraid you were going to elope."

"He said I reminded him of Ally McBeal. What an insult; she's a neurotic adolescent."

"You were a neurotic adolescent when he met you," she offered. "You were fourteen."

"Fifteen," I corrected. Everyone was expanding the time frame.

"At least she's skinny," my mother said.

I sent David a bunch of questions, which he answered right away. After a few cheerful e-mails back and forth, he wrote: "Here's my theory. By the end, I was just another commodity to be dealt with, to be tossed in the garbage when you were finished with me."

No wonder he was a dentist, he always could draw blood. "You were never a commodity I tossed in the garbage," I wrote back, sincerely. "I loved you too much, I couldn't breathe without you. I was so tangled up senior year of college. I wanted to marry you and have a baby even though I hated the idea of marriage and motherhood . . ." I so wanted him to understand. ". . . I think I caused the entire disaster so I could get out . . . If we were together, I wouldn't have been able to leave . . ."

After spilling another page of confessionals, I requested a date. I offered to fly to Toronto for the day since it was only an hour-and-a-half plane ride, or asked if he'd come east. I was a travel-phobe, already exhausted by my marathon quest to remeet my former men. I really wanted him to come to New York.

"You like basketball? I'll get you court seats for the Knicks, or take you to Le Cirque . . ." I ended my missive, "Let me know. Thanks for helping me." In the morning I eagerly checked my e-mail and found his reply:

> Damn it, you are the same pain in the ass you always were,
> maybe worse. Our first conversation was fun, now I'm
> nauseous. You are an emotional vampire, sucking the feeling
> out of everyone you know (knew). Jesus Christ, what did it
> take you, three e-mails to dredge up the sewage (sue-age, as I
> used to call your internal castaways). I didn't give you what
> you wanted twenty-four years ago, why would I do it now?
> Dinner at Le Cirque, courtside seats, what is this, *Let's Make a
> Deal*? It feels more like *Antiques Roadshow*. Forget the reunion.
> I would rather take out my own appendix with a bottle of
> Jack and a dull spoon.

12

Everything easy I did early: growing breasts, wearing makeup, writing passionate love letters, smoking, and drinking. At thirteen, I snuck into the local bowling alley bar with my fake ID, sipped rum and diet Cokes, all five foot seven, 123 pounds of me disco dancing in tight leather pants and a halter. My cherry lip gloss left rings around the filters of my Pall Malls, a preteen middle-aged divorcée.

To keep the sordid truth from my parents, I needed the guise of social respectability. At fourteen, I joined the local youth organization of B'nai B'rith. Probably designed to keep teens like me out of trouble, it offered educational and charity functions to Jewish kids from the Midwest and Canada. I quickly rose through the ranks to become president of Aliyah, the West Bloomfield girls' chapter. In Hebrew the word *aliyah* meant to go up to the bimah, or stage, of the synagogue. Also, those who emigrated to Israel were said to be "making aliyah," which became the code the guy chapters used for getting to third base with a Bloomfield princess. I first heard of David in the fall of 1975. We were both spending the weekend at Camp Tamarack, a hundred-acre farm two hours north of the suburbs, for a fall religious retreat I hoped to turn into a sex-drugs-and-rock-and-roll spree.

As Aliyah's popular leader, I was trusted by all the girls. They brought me their problems. On Saturday night a new young member named Annie came to me, crying. Annie's trauma involved being taken advantage of by one David Green, a seventeen-year-old boy in the Canadian male chapter, Herzl. (They were named after Theodor Herzl, the founder of modern Zionism.) According to Annie, she and David had skipped out of the Shabbat service Friday night and sneaked to the lake. There he got her drunk on a bottle of stolen Manischewitz, took her clothes off, and almost talked her into going all the way. Worse, he then had the nerve to ignore her all Saturday.

Annie, in tears, pointed him out in the back of the dining room. I marched up to this brazen troublemaker and tapped him on the shoulder. "I hear you're the heathen out to seduce my whole chapter."

He turned around. He was wearing torn jeans and a flannel shirt. He had big shoulders. He was five ten, my father's height, with curly reddish hair like my mother. He had brown eyes that looked right through you.

"And who, pray tell, are you? The queen mother?" He was snide for a Herzl; the rest of the Canadian guys were exceedingly polite. I liked that he wasn't the least bit intimidated by me.

"I'm Sue, the president of Aliyah," I said. "Why are you playing mind games with Annie? All she did was like you."

"Mind games? She's been following me around like a lost puppy. Last night she begs me to take a walk to the lake. She throws off her clothes to go skinny dipping, then freaks out when I kiss her," he said, looking at my breasts, which were jiggling in a skin-tight white tube top. "Not that I owe you any explanation." He lit a Marlboro and offered me one, as if he knew I smoked.

"Well, she's upset. Her parents just got divorced, she's thirteen years old and confused. Why don't you talk to her? Tell her she's cute and nice but you're involved with someone else."

"Aye-aye, sir," he said. But his eyes softened as he lit my cigarette with a silver lighter.

I watched from the door as he went over to her table and put his arm around Annie. They talked for a long time. I was afraid he'd changed his mind and decided to like her. He didn't speak to either of us the rest of the weekend, but I caught him checking me out a few times. As we boarded the bus taking us back to our suburban headquarters on Sunday night, David kissed me good-bye. On the lips. He mentioned the address of a Herzl party in Southfield the next weekend.

I showed up at the party, which was sponsored by another girls' chapter, Disraeli. (Named for Benjamin, the British statesman.) It was being held in some Disraeli member's basement. The Disraeli chapter was our archrival, so I went downstairs quietly. The party was crowded. I saw David, nodded hello. Within half an hour we were dry humping in the hall closet. He was aggressive, big hands everywhere. He said his father owned a meat-packing plant he worked at in the summertime and he was used to slinging sides of beef. I was sick of polite Bloomfield boys who asked permission to kiss me. I liked that David was crude—it turned me on. Envisioning my future as a woman with a past, I desperately wanted to lose my virtue. But he scared me. Like Annie, I pushed him away. He pulled me back closer, slipping his hands under my shirt and kissing me harder. Just then some girl opened the door on us and yelled, "I told you not to let Aliyah crash our parties!"

He drove me home in his silver Camaro. It had an orange-and-black stripe down the hood, white Canadian plates, and a Bob Dylan bootleg in the cassette player. Unlike me, he was a confident driver. I'd never heard of Dylan or bootlegs before.

"Listen," he told me.

In the love song, the guy tells his girlfriend that he likes "the smile in your fingertips," the way "you move your hips," and "the cool way you look at me." In the last line he says that everything about her is bringing him misery.

"His voice sucks," I said.

Our contradictions appeared to match. I was an all "A" student, a cheerleader at a private school who would rather get stoned alone and read confessional poetry. My irreverent, rambling Romeo was a sharp pre-med from a nice Jewish family in Windsor, Ontario, forty-five minutes away from West Bloomfield. We'd go to rock concerts at a nearby outdoor stadium called Pine Knob, and parties where we'd drink vodka, smoke hash, and drop Quaaludes. He had a weird sense of humor, describing me as his "old sea hag," who had "violent eyes and breeder's hips," which for some reason, in the fall of 1976, seemed to me hysterical.

For my fifteenth birthday he bought me a gold heart necklace. Instead of a card there was a note, handwritten on his brown stationery. It was lines from a Dylan song. This one was about a lonely rich girl who goes to a fancy private school, but "only used to get juiced in it." Was he sending me a message? Both David and Dylan's words hit too close, working on different levels.

One muggy August midnight we parked at Orchard Lake, two miles from my parents' house. Lakes were our hotels in those days. We smoked a thick joint of strong Jamaican and made out on a blanket spread on the damp sand. I slapped a mosquito on my arm—too many bugs outside. The small speedboats docked by the pier rocked and swayed in the murky water, casting long, eerie shadows. I'd never been in love before. I was terrified that he didn't feel the same way.

"I'm not so good at emotional connections," I admitted.

"Let's just have a physical one," he said. "I don't like your personality anyway."

"Okay," I laughed, thinking what my mother had told me about sex: "First it hurts and you bleed. Then it gets better."

He grabbed me close and kissed me hard, his arm sneaking back to untie my halter.

"Not outside," I said. "We'll get bitten up."

We went into his backseat. I lay down, he got on top. He licked the inside of my ear. His skin was burning, coarse hands rubbing my breasts, legs, pulling down my jeans and black lace panties; I let him this time. I knocked my elbow on the door. He went for something in his wallet. "The rubber," he whispered, fumbling for a few seconds before he crawled back on top of me. I wrapped my legs around his waist and pulled his hair—I'd heard while you were doing it, guys liked when you pulled their hair. He took my hands, locking them over my head, and pushed into me. Then he collapsed on top. I couldn't move. My foot was falling asleep. Why was he stopping now?

"What happened?"

"I came."

"It's over?" I asked. "That's it?"

"You're not supposed to say that," he laughed. I saw the hideous baggy thing still on him. "I'm sorry. It was too fast." He'd done this before, I knew. "It gets better."

It didn't hurt, but maybe I was too stoned and missed it.

"At least I lost it," I said.

"Glad I could be of service." He opened the car door, stood up, and pulled the rubber off.

My thigh had some goo on it; I wiped it away. It was white, not red. "Are you sure we did it right? Mom said I was supposed to bleed." I got up too, pulled my jeans back on, and retied my halter. With my clothes on, I suddenly felt vulnerable. "Listen, if you don't really want to be together . . . I mean . . ." I started to say, but I was crying.

"Hey." He came closer, twirling a strand of my dark hair around his finger. "Do you think I'd put up with your insanity if I wasn't in love with you?"

I'd played out every possible scenario—one-night stand, platonic pain, eternal hatred—it had never occurred to me that our feelings could be mutual. Now what?

We did it all the time, everywhere. My mother and David were right, it got better. I liked it rough. Wearing only cowboy boots in his backseat or checking into a seedy motel in Ferndale for two hours. When no one was home one Saturday night, he came up to my room and without a word ravaged me on the pink carpet. Then he whispered, "I missed you."

Eventually my mother asked, "Have you been intimate with David?"

"You mean sex? Yeah, since last summer."

She cried for two weeks, then said, "Well, the Goodman women were always hot-blooded." (She evoked her maiden name in times of trauma.) I loved the way that sounded, as if I were suddenly a member of a secret Russian tribe. But then she kept worrying that David and I were going to run off and get married.

"Don't be silly. I'm only fifteen," I said, thinking it was cute that sex and marriage were so linked in her mind.

"I met your father when I was fifteen," she said proudly one night, serving David and my father brisket and lamb chops and spare ribs and potatoes. "David looks a little like him, don't you think?"

I wanted to marry him too, but chose my own metaphor. The rubbers he brought came in little blue plastic capsules. I collected the empties in a bag I kept in the basement. When he was gone I snuck down there and glued them together, making a blue plastic house. (My mother had chosen white brick, a garden in the front yard.)

The only thing I loved more than David was my acceptance to the University of Michigan, two years early. One piece of paper proved I was smart. I made copies for my father and brothers and kept the original in my purse. David was in grade thirteen, a Canadian requirement. I felt younger and older than him at the same time. Happily he had money, a car, and a hip father who encouraged his son's romps with an American college girl in the city my unhip father had deemed "The People's Republic of Ann Arbor."

Every Friday night of my freshman year, David showed up at my dorm room, bearing roses and presents: a T-shirt that said "Instant Foreplay," a charm bracelet with a gold "S" pendant lined with diamonds. Though I didn't like jewelry, I wore anything he gave me and kept the flowers on my dresser for weeks after they'd died. We'd usually kick my roommate out and crash together on the top bunk bed, which was too small for both of us, so we overlapped. I'd wind up on my stomach. He'd end up on his side, pushing against me.

My sophomore year he started college in London, Ontario, three hours farther away. I worried that he'd find a London girl. Yet I was his date for his kid brother's bar mitzvah at the Windsor Temple. I borrowed my mother's black satin dress. "Now that's a classy dame," his father said, winking at me, while all the Canadian cousins and uncles asked me to slow dance to "Sunrise, Sunset" and "You Are My Sunshine."

David seemed open and nonpossessive. He always said, "If you want, you can see other guys." I took that to mean I could fool around with anybody I felt like on weekdays, but I kept my weekends (and naked body) reserved for David. One Thursday afternoon, returning from a make-out session at Brad's, I found a letter under my door. It was lines from another Dylan song, this one about a girl sneaking off to somebody else's bedroom. I ended it with Brad.

The summer after my junior year, one of the blue-capsuled rubbers must have broken. My house came tumbling down. I was two weeks late. Six home pregnancy tests confirmed it. He said, "We could get married." I couldn't imagine having a baby in nine months, in May. My God, what would I do? I couldn't postpone getting my diploma. That would mean I wasn't smart after all.

My rational, selfish side took over. I booked an abortion, the first open appointment they had, two weeks later. It was on a Saturday. David drove me to a hospital in downtown Detroit and paid for it. I woke up from the anesthetic, hallucinating that the doctor standing over me was my father.

"Are you going to tell your mother?" David asked on the drive home.

"I'm not telling anyone." I was still groggy. I stared out the window at the blocks of torn-down buildings as he turned onto Northwest highway. It was a dark, rainy August day. Usually a speed freak, he was driving slowly.

"You hungry?" He reached into the paper bag between us and pulled out the triple-decker salami hero he'd bought for me at the hospital cafeteria. Since we'd found out, he'd been feeding me giant buckets of popcorn at the movies, bringing over fried chicken and pizza. I couldn't wait to get back to school to starve.

"No." I stuck out my tongue. He took a bite of the sandwich and got mustard on his chin. I wiped it off with a napkin.

"When do your classes start?" he asked. "When do you register?"

Usually a man of few words, he was trying too hard to make conversation; we'd switched roles. The new black snakeskin boots he'd given me for my birthday weren't worn in yet and they hurt my feet.

"Still want me to come up next weekend?" he asked, pulling into the driveway of my parents' white house. The porch light went on—my mother was home. I nodded, not sure. He didn't come in.

She opened the door. "Why didn't you invite David in? I put out some Nutter Butters."

"I have to go pack for school."

"I put a new nightgown in your room for you to take. Black, your favorite, I think it's morbid. Don't roll it up in a ball like you did last time."

"Thanks." I avoided her eyes, sure that it showed on my face.

The hot pink wallpaper in my childhood bedroom, which had seemed mod when I chose it at eight, made me dizzy. I went to the scale. I had gained nine pounds from all of David's food, as if he wanted to replace the loss, replenish me. I needed a shower but didn't want to take off my clothes. I picked up the nightgown, low-cut and lacy, just what I needed now, a sexy nightgown from my mother. I took the Percodan David gave me with diet soda.

Turning off the lights, I lay down on the hot pink bedspread. "We could get married," he'd said. But I didn't want to move to Canada, where David went to school. I wanted to live in Manhattan after I graduated. The big city was too much for a Windsor boy. To him *I* was the big city.

I heard a car pull up the driveway and ran to the window. I caught the flash of silver, hoping David had changed his mind and come back. But it was just my father's Cadillac. I felt empty, like I'd managed to lose my baby and my only lover in the same second. I lit a cigarette and turned up the new tape David gave me, though I couldn't quite make out the words. Something about "the guilty undertaker," a "lonesome organ grinder," and silver saxophones that say "I should refuse you . . ."

When David opened the door to my Ann Arbor apartment a week later, he walked into a loud, crowded party, everyone tripping on magic mushrooms. "Who are all these clowns?" he demanded. He was seething. He hated having a lot of people around, but I'd invited them anyway. We went to my bedroom. He tried to hold me but I didn't want to be sexual. I was still bleeding; nobody had told me you bled for ten days. I moved closer, just wanting to hug, and said, "Maybe we need time apart."

The Dead blasted on my roommate Nicole's stereo. I hated the Dead. Why was he leaving? I wanted him to leave. I'd never been so torn. After he walked out, I locked my door.

Everyone was gone in the morning, though the place was spotless, like nothing had happened. Nicole must have cleaned. I was sweating; the long nightgown my mother had given me was tangled around my thighs. The collar was too frilly; it made me itch. I ripped off a line of lace, the way religious Jews tore a piece of clothing to announce they were in mourning.

I didn't speak to David for six months. Then a letter came with lines from the song "Visions of Johanna." Another puzzle. It was about a girl named Louise, who was "delicate," "just near," and "seems like the mirror." But Louise only makes it clear to him that "Johanna's not here."

"Does this mean you still love me?" I called and asked him.

"It's complicated."

"David, it's me," I pleaded. "You can tell me . . ."

"Everything's ruined." He sounded tortured.

"It doesn't have to be ruined," I said.

But it was. In March I opened Nicole's drug drawer and found a letter on his brown stationery, in his handwriting. Addressed to Nicole. Dated October. Telling her how good she tasted. Nicole always said I could go into the drawer for joints. Had she left the stack of letters for me to find?

I sat down on her bed and read them, putting together the missing pieces of the last six months of my life. The night I locked him out of my bedroom he'd slept in Nicole's. All term he had been driving to Ann Arbor, checking into hotels with her: Campus Inn, the Bell Tower. One night our mutual friend Kyla had come along too. They all got stoned and had a threesome.

Everyone knew. Brad, who resented David, since he was the reason I wouldn't sleep with him, said, "You deserve it." My new sweet friend Tommy said, "Nobody deserves this." Claire said, "At least it's clear that it's over. Black and white. Susie, you have to move on." I couldn't eat for weeks.

In a surge of dim, misplaced energy, I aced finals, though I didn't go to graduation. On my last night in Ann Arbor, Nicole was gone. I couldn't stop picturing her at a local hotel with David. Next to the joints and letters was a bag of pills I washed down with vodka. I woke up on the floor, half dressed and feeling stupid that I'd managed to fail love, life, and suicide. My head was pounding as I packed my stuff in garbage bags and carried them out to my ugly orange Cutlass in the parking lot.

After my last trip, I locked the front door. Then I remembered to check the mail. Back inside I found one letter in the box, addressed to me, on official stationery. An acceptance to NYU's master's in English program. I'd forgotten I'd applied.

13

When I fled Ann Arbor after college, I thought I was rid of the Midwest and David forever. Nicole was a petite yet very large-busted Manhattan girl who boasted of her multiple orgasms. I assumed David would marry her. Instead he called me in New York to tell me it was over.

"When?" I asked, pretending not to care.

"The minute you found out," he said.

I penned a lurid short story called "Pieces," about a man who takes apart a woman. He rips out her brain, heart, and tear ducts and throws them to the floor. He keeps her hair, breasts, and vagina, detaching them from her torso to form the perfect woman. After putting her back together he makes love to the hollow shell, never hearing the haunting moans coming from under the bed. In the last line he coos, "Honey, this is the best it's ever been for me." It was my first published piece in New York, printed in NYU's literary magazine. I sent him a copy with the note "Thanks for the inspiration." He wrote back saying, "Your envelope was dripping blood. Glad you're happy in your new city."

One Saturday afternoon a year later, David showed up at my New York apartment. He said he had news to tell me: he'd been accepted to dental school in Toronto. "What do you really want to tell me?" I asked, expecting an apology. Instead he admitted that his life was falling apart. His father's business was in serious trouble and his parents were splitting up. I was shocked. I held him close, still in love, all ready to do something stupid, mistaking his sadness for the desire to reconcile. Then he mentioned his girlfriend, Eve, the quiet Canadian. She was moving to Toronto with him.

The last time I visited Canada was for my friend Howard's wedding in 1989. It was held at the Windsor Temple, where I'd been years before, for David's brother's bar mitzvah. David wasn't invited to the wedding, but on the wall I spied him in a group photograph of Herzl. It was taken at the Camp Tamarack Convention where we'd first met. It was as though he were staring at me, following me around the room. Something was wrong.

Sure he was nearby, I called his mother's home from the temple. She said, "David is in town this weekend. He went to Detroit. I'll tell him you called." He was in Detroit, I was in Windsor. We could have passed on the highway, it seemed almost destined. But he didn't return my call, false alarm. I caught the first plane back to New York. He phoned Sunday night.

"I was in West Bloomfield," he said. "You were all over the place."

"You should have called me." My heart was thrashing.

". . . I thought you were in New York. Figured you were married by now."

"Still single," I said. "Are you and Eve still . . ."

"She dumped me last week," he said. "I'm a wreck. That's why I came home last weekend, to clear my head. Wish I could have seen you . . . Will you fly to Toronto?"

He felt it too, it wasn't my imagination. "Are you nuts?" I said. "It took me almost ten years to get over you."

"You don't sound over me," he said, seductively. "Think about it. Let me know."

That week, in between going to therapy (Dr. G. said, "Don't even think about going to Toronto") and handing in three articles, I couldn't not think about it. The first flame that wouldn't die, like one of those trick birthday candles. Abortion, illicit affairs with my friends, years apart—nothing had killed it.

I called American Airlines. The ticket was only two hundred dollars if I went standby. I'd been crazy about this guy since I was a teenager. I was almost thirty and there was still something intense between us. Though I wasn't sure exactly what, I called to tell him yes.

"Hey. It's me," I said. "How's it going?"

"Crazy week." He sounded strange.

"Hard exams?"

"No. Eve came back. She had cold feet, went to her mother's. We're engaged."

"Congratulations." Tears fell so fast I didn't feel them coming.

"What's up?" he said.

"Oh, I found a small publisher for my poetry book. It's called *Internal Medicine*." I was lying. I hadn't even finished the manuscript, but I needed an excuse to be calling other than "I decided to marry you."

"We both had good news this week."

"Take care," I told him.

Howard mentioned, a few years later, that David and Eve's first son had died in infancy. I was still so self-involved and confused, for a second I feared it was punishment for the abortion I'd had senior year. Then I realized it was just lingering guilt, there was no connection at all.

Now nearly forty, married, obsessively analytic, and infertile, I wasn't satisfied with the "he done me wrong" version of the David story I'd been stuck on for two decades. From here it looked different, like a postmodern tragedy, filled with omens from the start: "Why are you playing mind games with Annie? All she did was like you," I'd asked him. The *Blood on the Tracks* bootleg. A silver car like my father's.

My mother met my father on the Lower East Side when she was fifteen. He was a pre-med student she found scruffy, "handsome like a gangster." I didn't believe her. She proved it with a worn 1947 picture of Dad, hanging out on Delancey Street in jeans and leather jacket, a cigarette dangling from his lips. She married him at nineteen and dropped out of college.

At nineteen I was mired in a big Freudian quandary. Stay in the Midwest to marry my own pre-med/tough guy, repeating my mother's life, or go east by myself. Afraid to simply walk out of the good girl role, I simulated a series of explosions to blast my way out. First I became pregnant right in time for it to interfere with graduation. "A smart girl like you couldn't figure out how to get on the pill?" Dr. G. asked, rhetorically.

I thought the abortion would scare David off for good. He surprised me by returning. The Friday night he came back, I planned a wild party so I wouldn't have to be alone with him. I bought the drugs, threw David at my friends Nicole and Kyla, who looked hot in their miniskirts and tight tank tops. I refused to touch him, then locked him out of my bedroom. "He could have just gone home," Dr. G. argued. "He didn't have to sleep with both of them."

But maybe he did. In my current zeal for antivictimization, I believed that I'd controlled it all subconsciously, I'd written the script. The last scene had to be unalterable and extreme enough to propel me out of the Midwest and change my fate. There was a huge payoff: escaping the role of housewife in Canada, which somehow seemed even worse than being a housewife in Michigan. After five years, leaving David behind would make me the bad guy. I knew he'd be enraged, he was the macho type who'd want revenge. If he slept with my girlfriends, he'd take all the heat and I could never touch him again.

A little farfetched, but I did get everything I wanted: the big city, a big career, a big New York man to marry me fifteen years later, when I was ready. I forgave Kyla (whom I wound up introducing to her husband) and Nicole, whom I bumped into in the ladies' room at an uptown charity fund-raiser a year after it happened. She pulled up her shirt to show me the scar from her breast reduction surgery and said, "Now they're perfect B's, just like yours." We all had scars.

I reread David's angry e-mail. Talk about dripping blood. At least one of my exes could still make me cry. From "fun ride" to agony in twenty-four hours. I went back through my sent mail to figure out what had provoked him. Was it casually starting a sentence: "Though I'm old and fat and wrinkled now"? I had desexed myself. I didn't even think it was true.

Just the other day a car full of teenage boys shouted "Xena! Xena!" when I walked by with my student Angie, aka HOTCHICK66.

"Who's Zena?" I asked.

"Warrior princess," she said. "Because of your bangs."

Perhaps it was selfish to e-mail the words: "I wanted to have the baby." Bringing up dead babies was a disgusting thing to do to someone who had lost a real child.

"Check out David's e-mail." I showed Aaron the printout when he came home. "He's right. I am an emotional vampire, calling after twenty years. No wonder he won't see me."

"He'll see you," Aaron said.

"He said I reminded him of Ally McBeal. The scrawny lawyer on that dumb TV show."

"A lot of guys find her sexy. They jack off to her." It seemed chivalrous—Aaron was defending my allure. David did marry a skinny girl.

"If an old girlfriend from high school wanted to see you, what would it take for you to get on a plane?" I asked.

"If she was dying," Aaron answered. "If she was truly desperate."

"It's only an hour and a half to Toronto," I said. "I could fly there and come back the same day. American Airlines is nine hundred dollars for a round-trip."

"Air Canada is cheaper," Aaron said. "When I went to Toronto to work on that Imax film, I came back the same day." He was being awfully helpful.

"I could fly in this Sunday, meet him for lunch at the airport, and fly back Sunday night," I mused.

"You could fuck him at the airport hotel," Aaron deadpanned, walking into the Bat Cave.

I recalled how, at Nicole's wedding, she'd met Aaron for the first time. She'd stared at him, then looked at me and said, "It's wild. He looks just like David."

"He does not," I'd said, indignant.

"Come on," she'd said. "They're both big, handsome guys with curly hair and brown eyes."

I went to my calendar and looked at Sunday, the day I had chosen to go to Toronto. It was day fourteen, I would be ovulating. Aaron looked like David, David's sperm worked. My God, was that why I needed to see David now? I wanted my baby back.

"D: Sorry if I offended/bombarded/upset you," I e-mailed the next day, when Aaron was at work, choosing my words carefully. Honest but vulnerable. I didn't want to lose David again, not just yet. There were still things I had to know. "I spent years writing a novel I couldn't sell. I felt like a total failure. I decided to forget it and have a baby, but I failed at that too." Though I was being manipulative, the truth of those lines got to me and tears welled up in my eyes. "For some reason, writing about my past seems healing and redemptive. You're the last person I need to see. It's so ludi-crous and unfair I was throwing out anything (basketball, Le Cirque) to get you here. I never travel, never offered to get on a plane and come back the same day for anyone. I'm desperate. I feel like I'm screwing this up too, like if I could be light and breezy or appear rich and successful, you might see me. I have to stop crying now and go teach my class. S"

After I sent the message I also sent a message to Claire, whose father could sometimes get courtside season tickets for the Knicks. I'd come up with a potential new ending. I'd get a pair of tickets for David and his eleven-year-old. They'd meet me in front of Madison Square Garden, where I'd hand him the tickets and see his son. We'd chat casually for a few minutes, no big deal. Then I'd walk downtown alone. Having remet all my old boyfriends, my six-month heartbreak journey would officially be over. First love, last good-bye.

14

SUBJ: Sorry
DATE: Thursday Nov. 16, 7:39 A.M.
FROM: Dr.dg@ltd.com
TO: Profsue123@aol.com

Sue: Here's a Kleenex, blow your nose and straighten up.
Christ, we've both been through a lot since we parted. It
doesn't matter if we don't see each other. I'll be the one who
won't meet you after twenty years. I am answering your
questions in between patients.
1. Question: Do you still have hair?
Answer: Yes, I have hair, a little thin on top, but it's there.
2. Question: Do you wear jeans or are you a total suit?
Answer: When I got out of school and started making
money I bought ten suits. I realized I looked ridiculous and
went back to jeans, T-shirts, and leather jackets. And I can't
believe the way you described yourself—you always were a
drama queen.
3. Question: How do you remember me from high school?
Answer: As a smart, witty, popular girl in control of the "in
crowd." The fact that I was with you for so long gave me a

mystique. I guess because of the way you chewed through guys back then. I was cool because I was with you. You were also a giant bag of need.

4. Question: Do you still listen to Dylan?

Answer: No, I was thinking of selling my old bootleg collection on eBay.

5. Question: Were you as badly hurt as I was? If so, do I owe you an apology?

Answer: With you it had to end bloody. But tell me this: If it was such a nuclear holocaust, why did you stay friends with Nicole and Kyla? Why didn't you hang up when I called you in New York? You got what you wanted. I wasn't in pain. I had a great time. Stop apologizing for your life.

6. Question: Have you seen any of my writing?

Answer: Look, you made it. You said you write for *The New York Times* and *Washington Post.* Why do you need my applause?

7. Question: Why don't you want to see me? Are you scared?

Answer: I want to. At some point I'll fly in with my son— he's a huge basketball fan. For now, let's leave the bad memories intact. Am I scared to see you again? You're fucking right I am. Think you're still nuts? Is a trout's ass watertight? Can we finish with the joint therapy session now? Come on girl, let it go. It's time.

15

Whenever I was bored or on a losing streak, I pulled out my spiral notebook and made Love Charts. These were in-depth, full-page diagrams listing all my boyfriends over the years who I had said "I love you" to who had said it back. (After careful deliberation, Brad's, "If I was capable of loving someone it would be you," was deemed eligible.) These were the guys I'd really cared about, the home team. Next to their names, I wrote their age, height, current job, best assets, fatal flaws, preference for makeout music, and duration of our relationship. I was trying to make it rational, analyze the stats, and see the exact point where I went wrong.

Now, after my monumental feat of reconnecting—and surviving—my five most horrible rejections, I regressed to that obsessive teenage chart-making habit. I added Aaron to the bottom of the master list (see chart 1). The last entry. The game was over, results were in. I was sure the recap would be illuminating. This was the master list, which, I was sure, would reveal The Final Relationship Truth.

I studied my map of men for hours, searching for patterns. It appeared that, over the years, the partners I picked became older and more urban. Or was that just because I was aging myself, in

Manhattan? The trajectory seemed to show them getting less religious and more artsy. This was a good sign, since I'd become a godless cynic whose only authority figures were my editors and my analyst. It seemed I was much more apt to be completely heartbroken when I was at my thin weight. Conversely, I had happily pranced down the aisle at my heaviest. So when I gave up all the dieting and exercising, there was room to fit in happiness.

In the last column I calculated ratios on the heartbreak scale, which was disheartening. In terms of the 1–10 scoring, a 2 or 3 meant I was upset for a few months. Anything over an 8 1/2, I was catatonic and had to sit shiva. Four guys on the heartbreak scale (David, Brad, George, and Richard) were straightforward slaughters, between 9 and 10. Tom was much more complicated.

He'd nicked me lightly in college, when he'd said, "You're in deeper than I am" (2), and struck a second blow when he moved back to California and wouldn't speak to me (2). Then last summer, seventeen years later, he hurt, confused, and flipped me out in a fresh way I'd never imagined (5). So in my estimation of emotional damage inflicted, Tom was right up there with the best of them, pulling in a 9 altogether.

According to my Time Line (see chart 2), it had taken David five years to amass a 10 when I was fifteen to nineteen. Both Richard and George rose to 9 1/2s in half that period. This seemed significant, heartbreaking within itself. I had two degrees, years of therapy with a fabulous analyst, and read books constantly. I desperately needed to believe I'd gotten wiser. Yet as I aged, my feelings were hurt just as much as before, but in fewer years.

On the plus side, there was less male overlap as I entered my thirties, which meant I got tired of triangles, or perhaps just tired of Brad (who'd overlapped the most). When I once showed Dr. G. a current Love Chart, she pinpointed signs of improvement. Getting out of one bad relationship at a time faster, it turned out, was excellent progress.

I was thrilled I kept plugging away until I found Aaron. He embodied all the qualities I was attracted to in his predecessors—combined in one person, my own male evolution. As in that first short story I published, "Pieces," I'd taken parts of old boyfriends to create the perfect husband. Yet how would I know if our marriage would last when half of them dissolved into divorce? I wondered if Elizabeth Taylor made charts of her ex-husbands.

In my mother's kitchen last summer, I asked my parents the secret to their happy forty-six-year union. "It's a crapshoot," my father said, taking a bite out of an oversize oatmeal raisin cookie. "We got lucky," my mother said, wiping the crumbs from his shirt.

LOVE CHART #1

	(WHEN WE MET)						
Guy	His Age	His Height	My Age	My Weight	Duration	Nickname	Assets
David	17	5'10½"	15	123	5 yrs.	*Root Canal*	car, cowboy boots, Dylan tickets
Brad	18	6'	16	126	on/off 15 yrs.	*Mr. Studrocket*	shoulders
Tom	22	5'11"	19	128	3½ yrs.	*Beach Boy*	legs
Richard	35	5'11"	24	129	1½ yrs.	*The Biographer*	Village apartment, hair, Dylan book
George	28	6'	28	123	1½ yrs.	*Hamlet*	joystick, Village apartment
Aaron	43	6'4"	33	134	8 yrs. (so far)	*Batman*	hair, height, brains, Dylan bootlegs

LOVE CHART #2

Age: 13 - 14 - 15 - 16 - 17 - 18 - 19 - 20 - 21 - 22 - 23 - 24 - 25 - 26 -

DAVIDDAVIDDAVIDDA

TOMTOMTOMT

BRADBRADBRADBRADBRADBRADBRADBRAD

RICHARDRIC

Year: 74 - 75 - 76 - 77 - 78 - 79 - 80 - 81 - 82 - 83 - 84 - 85 - 86 - 87 -

Fatal Flaw	Sex Music	Current Job	Current Status	Heartbreak Level
ego	*Blood on the Tracks*	periodontist	married w/ 1 kid in Toronto	10
ego	Kinks/Cars	biology prof., author	single in Boston	10
lack of ego	Joni Mitchell	lawyer	divorced w/ 1 kid in L.A.	$2 + 2 + 5 = 9$
ego, dog	*Blood on the Tracks*	biographer	divorced & remarried w/1 kid in Westchester	$9^1/_2$
lack of ego	Bob Marley	theater prof.	married w/ 1 kid in Brooklyn	$9^1/_2$
slob	*Blood on the Tracks*	TV/film writer	married (to me) in NYC	undetermined

7-28-29-30-31-32-33-34-35-36-37-38 - 39 - 40

```
          G
          E
          O
          R
          G
          E  G
             E
BRADBRAD  O
          R
          G  AARONAARONAARONAARONAARONAAR
          E
```

8-89-90-91-92-93-94-95-96-97-98-99-2000-2001

16

Batman Returns

A week before New Year's, something strange occurred. I fell in love with my husband again. I don't know how it happened. As we were walking home from a holiday party, he took my hand at Forty-third Street and Fifth Avenue, in front of the public library. He stuck out his other hand and commandeered a yellow cab.

"I can't believe you found a taxi tonight," I said, feeling happy as he opened the door for me. The happiness startled me. In that moment everything about him seemed destined: his height, his messy mop of hair, the black leather jacket I'd bought him. After my late tango with five old lovers, I was choosing him again. He was the only one I wanted to father the child we couldn't figure out a way to have.

After trying to conceive, and failing for so long, I was ready to get aggressive, with fertility drugs or in-vitro or whatever else it would take. When I sensed his resistance, I began resenting Aaron's defective sperm, as if he'd slowed it down intentionally. He worked slowly, got ready to go out slowly, told jokes slowly, liked to make love slowly. It had taken him three years of courting me to cough up a ring—at age forty-six. It figured that his sperm was snail-paced. How could it not be? Recently, when he'd been a half hour late to meet me for dinner, he'd said, "There's a Zen saying I like, 'When late, walk slower.'"

"Here's a Sue saying. When you're late for me, run," I'd told him.

"You don't blame me for my slow sperm, do you?"

"Of course not, sweetie," I'd said, kissing him.

My gynecologist recommended Aaron see a urologist. After tests, the urologist said that Aaron's problem was varicocele, a varicose vein in the testicles that interferes with sperm development. He recommended an operation on Aaron's penis. Aaron refused, but I wasn't giving up. A new fertility specialist suggested another blood workup on me. Uh-oh. I only loved blood as a metaphor. Although there was nothing lower than my writing workshop's taunt: "There's no blood here," the real stuff freaked me out.

A doctor's daughter, I was an eternally squeamish patient, fainting at pinky blood tests and avoiding appointments until emergencies. Once a year I went to Dr. Cherry, the gynecologist, who'd won me over by talking about his four baby-book deals, autographing his latest hardcover right after my last Pap smear.

I had found a way to rectify the frustration of my childhood and change the rules of "The Disease Game," played relentlessly by my father and brothers. I only saw doctors who talked about writing! Engaged in a conversation in my language, I was calmer, distracted from my fears about what their intrusive instruments were doing.

My dentist (whom I ran to only when something hurt or fell out of my mouth) told me, while replacing a broken crown, that Dana Carvey was his patient and they were cowriting a sitcom about a dentist whose worst patient was the stand-up comic Dana Carvey. When he heard I was a writer, my ophthalmologist (whom I found when I was near blind with a double stye) told me about his mystery novel, set in Russia, where the microfiche was hidden in the spy's eye.

*   *   *

For the new blood tests, I lay down and bravely let the nurse (who had written rhyming sonnets in high school) take twelve vials of my blood. Then I went home and slept for twenty-four hours. Unfortunately, the results, which came a week later, showed that Aaron and I were both carriers of Tay-Sachs, a deadly Jewish genetic disease. That meant, even if Aaron agreed to the operation he refused to have and I got knocked up naturally, there was one chance in four that our baby would die in infancy. What a cruel joke. It took me twenty years to nail a brilliant Jewish guy with whom I could go forth and multiply, when any uncircumcised prick in the world could offer a child with a life span.

Whether or not the kid carried the disease could only be determined at twenty weeks of pregnancy, by an amniocentesis, which involved inserting a long needle into my uterus. If that wasn't scary enough, there was a tiny chance the amnio could miss it and I'd give birth to a baby with brain degeneration. Instead of taking that risk, all our doctors suggested that Aaron and I bypass any chance of the Tay-Sachs by trying artificial insemination with a sperm donor.

The sperm donation would be anonymous and Aaron would be the child's father—legally, emotionally, and financially. (He'd have to sign a form.) He wouldn't be connected to the child genetically, but in my mind he was already my child's daddy.

I called a fertility specialist to make a date for us to visit her sperm clinic uptown, which was called "Repro X." It sounded like a twenty-four-hour Kinko's, only what we wanted to reproduce was us. I pictured standing in line and putting in an order for the biological seeds for my children.

"What does the 'X' stand for?" I wondered out loud, as we got ready for our appointment. "Isn't the X chromosome the one that's responsible for femaleness? Shouldn't it be 'Y'?"

"Extraterrestrial," Aaron said. "We'll have a martian."

I thought of ex, as in old boyfriend, which was intriguing, though I felt vindicated and finished with all of them. Then I recalled a term from a seventh-grade math class I had flunked: exponent. I looked it up and read Aaron the meaning: "a symbol denoting the power to which the latter is raised."

"A symbol of my failure," he said.

"If my eggs were the problem, I would get a donor in a second," I said. "Will you get dressed already? I don't want to be late."

"If we take the subway we'll be early," he said.

"We will not," I argued. "It never comes on time."

We took the subway to Eighty-sixth Street and Lexington Avenue, arriving ten minutes ahead of schedule. While waiting, the receptionist handed us a "Donor Selection List." It was amazingly similar to my Love Chart. Instead of names, the guys had numbers. They were categorized by height, weight, body frame, skin, hair and eye color, religious/ethnic background, occupation, and blood type. Though my final column was "Heartbreak scale," their final column was "Pregnancy." A check meant that the guy's sperm had already impregnated at least one of Repro X's customers. I wanted to be next.

The doctor called us into her office, pictures of her two young children on the desk. She had dark brown hair and looked my age. She asked about our preferences. I knew what I wanted: a replica of Aaron. My dream DNA would, as closely as possible, create another six-foot-four comedy writer with brown eyes, curly hair, and sardonic wit. She stared at Aaron, then typed into a computer. She was playing cybermatchmaker.

"I have five potentials who resemble Aaron," she said, explaining that we could buy twenty-page "extensive donor profile" packets, fifteen dollars each, to "get to know them better."

Aaron wrote a check for $475, which included $400 for her fee and $75 for the top-five contenders. Both David and Tommy had paid $400 for my abortions. I always made men pay for my problems with fertility, as if it was their fault I got pregnant. Or not.

In the cab downtown, I breezed through the questionnaires, which listed an extraordinary wealth of information (including cause of death of paternal and maternal grandparents); medical questions (Ever have hepatitis B? A sexually transmitted disease? Jaundice? Cleft lip or palate? They had all circled no); physical characteristics (shoe size, nose width, freckles, dimples); and personal likes and dislikes (favorite sport, color, food, music—none chose Dylan). At home we sat across from each other in the living room and read through them carefully.

It felt like a parody of the modern mating scene. I'd been in love five times. Now I was going on five genetic blind dates—minus the meeting, relationship, sex, and marriage, skipping right to procreation. Only this time, my husband would be choosing—or nixing—my match.

"This Russian guy, number 023, looks good. He's twenty-two, in graduate school," I said. "Brown curly hair and tall, like you."

"I'm not having a Russian cabdriver!" Aaron said, putting number 023's packet in the reject pile.

"Okay. Next. Number 025. Curly brown hair. American. Speaks two languages. He wants to be a comedy writer," I read.

"Let's see." Aaron grabbed the report from my hands. "Look, this guy checked that he smokes cigarettes occasionally and tried marijuana a few times. That means he's a chain-smoking druggie like you. Forget it. It's a conspiracy."

"He's just being more honest than the other ones."

"I never smoked anything," Aaron bragged. "Look. Not one of his answers are the least bit funny."

Great, now he was getting competitive with the pamphlets.

"It's not a *Saturday Night Live* audition. Nobody's funny answering a medical survey," I said. "They do it for money. It's not like I'm gonna have sex with them."

"I would be funny," Aaron said.

"I know. I really want it to be you. But it's anonymous . . . Unless you want to get more information about that operation the doctor mentioned."

"My penis is not having an operation!" Aaron raised his voice. He was as scared of doctors as I was, though I had a better excuse, growing up with them. "I've already jerked off in a cup five times," he reminded me.

"I know, honey." I patted his head.

He'd told me that at the urologist's office, instead of *Penthouse,* he'd used a picture of me. The ultimate declaration of love. My sexual fantasies still tended toward hulking strangers. Aaron was right, men were more romantic.

I read through the third pamphlet, number 054. "American. A lawyer, six foot three. He never smoked anything."

"So he says. Why so tall?" Aaron asked. "What if it's a girl? She'll be six foot two. I hate lawyers. What if she's a six-foot-two lawyer?"

"You do not hate lawyers. Your father was a lawyer."

"A judge," Aaron corrected.

"He was a lawyer first!" I shook my head. "The fourth one, number 063, is a medical student, five eleven, American, non-smoking. Find something wrong with this one." I handed it to him.

"His grandfather died at forty-nine."

I looked at the page. "Read the next line. It says his grandfather was a prisoner in Siberia!"

"Another Russian!"

"The donor isn't Russian, he was born here. Both our families are from Russia! That's our problem. We're probably cousins." I looked through the fifth one, number 086. "He's American born, American parents. American grandparents. He's a teacher. Twenty-nine years old."

"He's too old."

"You're fifty. How is twenty-nine too old?"

"I'm too old," Aaron said. "To be a father." He turned through the pages and pointed. "Look at his reasons for doing this. 'Giving life is a miracle.' He's a religious fanatic."

"What's he supposed to say on a questionnaire? I'm broke and sperm sells better than blood?"

"I can't help it, I hate all of them," he said.

" 'Cause they're not you?"

This was exactly what I detested most about marriage. I could not make one simple decision about my own apartment, taxes, or womb without getting his sign-off. I felt like blindly choosing a packet and getting inseminated next week when Aaron wasn't looking. I'd decided it would be sinful to try to trick Aaron into having an old lover's baby. Yet couldn't one trick one's husband into having the baby of a stranger?

"I thought you were open to this. What's going on?"

"I don't want to have a child," my husband said. "I told you that when we met."

17

Claire was right, you are beautiful," Aaron Levin said when I stepped out of the elevator into my apartment lobby, where I'd told him to meet me. I was on deadline, not at all in the mood for a fix-up. At least he was tall. A comedy writer, Claire had said. She'd met Aaron when she'd come to pick up Hans from the strike line at the Writer's Guild, where Hans and Aaron had bonded over root beer and residuals. Claire and Hans were blissfully engaged at the time, so she was on a campaign to find me a fiancé.

"Good opener." I led Aaron out of my building quickly so that my doorman, Juan, the busybody, wouldn't hear. "How about Chinese?" I suggested. It was fast and cheap. I had a thousand-word review of a long Holocaust memoir due the next day. "Sun Chu Mey is on Ninth Avenue."

"There's a great Japanese next door."

It figured he'd choose the slower, more expensive place. His glasses had thick lenses. He was braino-looking, like my brothers. He dressed in their big, schleppy guy style—flannel shirt untucked, the bottom of his jeans frayed, worn white sneakers that made him look like an oversized kid.

"I heard you wrote a humor book," I said.

He waited at the light though no cars were coming. I crossed ahead of him.

"You walk too fast," he told me.

"You walk too slow."

"I edited a humor book," he said.

I saw one of the old dog people across the street, Fifi's owner, who waved. I looked at my date, deciding whether I wanted to be seen with him. He was good looking in a comfortable way, familiar— I could have known him forever. At the restaurant I picked a table in front and draped my blazer over the chair.

"You don't seem funny," I said.

"Give me a chance to warm up." He took a sip of water.

"Tell me about your book. What's the title?"

"Are you hungry?" he asked.

"Are you nonlinear?" I took a sip of water too and opened the menu. " 'Cause I'm always literal."

"*Junk Food*," he said. "It's an anthology. I was the editor. I commissioned eighty comedy writers to write about their favorite fast food."

"Fantastic idea."

"That's what I thought." He ordered sake for two, how presumptuous. I changed my order to diet soda, but the waiter said the machine was broken. I put my blazer back on.

"Be right back." I ran to the deli on the corner to get two cans of diet Coke. "I need a glass with ice," I told the waiter upon my return. He brought it, eyeing me suspiciously, as if I'd just sneaked in a pint of cheap vodka. I poured the soda and took a sip, hiding the can on the floor.

"A woman who knows what she wants," Aaron said. He looked like he was unsure whether buying my own soda was cute or emasculating.

I picked the safest cooked thing on the menu—chicken teriyaki.

He ordered pieces of sashimi—spicy tuna, eel, and octopus. Uh-oh, another food nut.

"How did the book do?" I asked.

"Not so well. All the publicity got screwed up. On the book tour we found stores all over the country had put it in the cooking section."

"That's hysterical."

"You don't laugh," he said. "You're the type who says, 'That's hysterical.' "

"I get the joke."

"What if I need an audience?" He looked in my eyes; he was serious.

"Don't stop in the middle of a good story. Come on. Your book tour was plunging into the sewer . . ." I said and he laughed loudly, to show me the kind of laughter he wanted me to have.

"Okay," he continued. "My life is in the sewer. I just had a bad fight with my old girlfriend, Lori, and I was . . ."

"Is she petite?" I asked.

"Yes. An ex-ballet dancer." He nodded. "You want to hear the story or not? . . . So I'm broke. Distraught about my career. I come out of the subway and see this bag lady selling books on a card table. I look over. Sure enough, she had a stack of mine. I went over, pointed to *Junk Food*, and asked what every writer would want to know: 'How's it doing?' She said, 'The book's doing great. It's one of my best sellers. Everyone loves the recipes.' " He laughed at his own punch line.

He wasn't yuck-yuck funny, he was self-deprecating. He was a louder laugher than I was, but otherwise shyer. I wished that he hadn't interjected his old girlfriend, Lori, into the conversation. Bad sign. Maybe he was still in love with her.

"That's a riot."

"That not laughing could be a problem," he said.

"Claire said you freelance for *Saturday Night Live*? How'd you get it? What if they offer you a full-time staff writer job? Would you take it?" I was asking too many questions.

"Probably not," he said. "I'm too old to do coke and sleep on my office floor."

"How old are you?"

"Forty-three," he answered. "Too old for you?"

"Depends how old you act."

"Twelve and a half." He smiled.

"You picked an interesting age. It's pre–bar mitzvah, before you were a man."

He stopped smiling. "I hate shrink talk," he said.

The waiter showed up with our food. I had to admit that Aaron's order, spread out on a wooden board, looked lovely.

"You have to taste," he told me.

"I've been told I have the most unsophisticated palate in the country."

"Who said that?" He poured soy sauce, mixing in light green goo. "Old boyfriend?"

"Richard." If he could throw Lori into the game, I'd raise him with Richard.

"You order the least expensive thing on the menu and bring your own drink. Did Richard say you were a cheap date?"

"Not emotionally."

He nodded, taking it in slowly, dipping a rainbow roll in his muddy soy concoction, eating it in one bite. "Why did he say your palate was unsophisticated?"

"I like iceberg lettuce and drink ten diet sodas a day. Claire calls it JAP juice." What a dumb thing to say. Show him I'm sexist and self-hating in the same sentence.

"Tell me about Richard." He lifted another roll between his chopsticks and offered it to me. I shook my head.

"Tell me about Lori." I finished the first soda, poured the

second. The teriyaki wasn't bad. I offered him a forkful. He took it freely.

"It's good," he said. "Lori and I split four months ago but we stayed friends."

"You still talk to her?" I jumped in too fast. It was our first date, none of my business.

"Not that often," he said.

"What does she do?"

"A shrink."

Now I laughed out loud, uproariously. "Don't tell me. You're not in therapy."

"Try the eel." He put a roll in my mouth. I took a bite, luckily getting mostly rice.

"You can stop laughing now," he said.

"Why did you split? She wanted to get married and have kids and you didn't?"

"How about red bean ice cream?" he asked.

"Already trying to poison me?" I signaled the waiter, who left the check on the table, between us. I reached for it.

He grabbed it first. "She wanted to get married and have kids and I didn't," he conceded, paying with cash.

Outside, I lit a cigarette, then asked, "Mind if I smoke?" It was a test: if a guy bothered me about smoking, I never went out with him again.

"My first lover was a smoker," Aaron said. "So I associate cigarettes with sex."

Good answer. It made me picture him in bed with some bohemian nymphet.

Walking around the West Village, I took Aaron's arm and led him past George's Jane Street building. I always looked for George in the top window, though I knew he'd moved to Brooklyn. Then we walked by the brownstone where Richard and I used to live. I still expected to see Richard on the stoop with Oscar, who'd growl at any male dogs in the vicinity. I usually zigzagged around the haunted street of exes. Being with Aaron made it less creepy. Like a journalist doing an in-depth profile, I kept asking questions, gathering background data. He grew up in Westchester, the New York equivalent of West Bloomfield. Aaron's mother was a housewife who was too smart to be a housewife. His father was a judge. Instead of the doctor-father-God syndrome, he was a victim of the judge-father-God version, everything revolving around the anointed father's profession. His sister still lived near his parents. Aaron and I were both the black sheep.

"How about dinner Wednesday?" He slipped his arm around my waist. "Indian?"

"Okay. But you're really pushing the exotic food thing." I was happy I wouldn't have to wait to see if he liked me. I never could stomach the anxiously-sitting-at-home-for-his-call part of it.

At the door I went to give him a peck on the lips, but we started really kissing. He was a great kisser. I had to stand on my toes to reach his face. He hugged me hard, then squeezed. I liked his grip, but I didn't let him in. I was thirty-two, with five bad breakups under my belt. It was enough, I'd decided, for one lifetime.

The next day, right after I faxed my one-thousand-word Nazi review, I had a flash that Aaron was going to be my husband. In the past there were men I thought I might marry, but there was never anybody I *knew* I would marry before. The phone rang. I could tell it was him. I bet he'd read my mind.

"I have to cancel our dinner Wednesday," he said. "I got a job offer."

"To be on *Saturday Night Live* full time?" I asked.

"No. *Seinfeld.* I'm moving to L.A."

"I thought I was the one with fear of intimacy." When he didn't laugh I realized he wasn't kidding. "When?"

"Tomorrow morning," he said.

18

Aaron took the job in California, so our relationship was over before it began. It figured I'd decide to marry a man who was leaving the state after our first date. At least I'd sidestepped another heartache. I had it down to a science: if you never fell in love, you never had to fall out of it.

A week later he left two messages. "I'm in L.A. I have a headache. I'll call tomorrow," the first one said. The second was equally ambivalent: "I couldn't sleep but I don't feel well so don't call back." Was that "I miss you" in Aaron-speak? I ignored both messages, so his next one was nicer. "I hate L.A. but I have frequent-flier miles if you want to visit." He didn't tell me not to call him back this time. I called him back but he wasn't there. We were courting by phone machine. I left the message "I'd love to come to L.A. for a weekend." Now that we were long distance and a real relationship was impossible, I felt much closer to him.

I made a reservation to fly to L.A. the following Friday. I called to tell him. As I was leaving a message, he picked up.

"You're coming this Friday?" He was taken aback. "I thought you had to work."

"I'm writing a profile but I can finish it out there," I said, excited to plan a trip on the sperm of the moment, as Claire called it. "I'll take a cab from the airport."

"No you won't." He stopped me. "What time does the flight get in? I'm picking you up. By the baggage claim."

At LAX Aaron came up to claim me, taking my bag out of my hand. I'd pictured a passionate airport makeout, but he pecked me on the cheek, as if I were an old aunt. I took off my blazer, showing off the low-cut black T-shirt I'd worn without a bra. I lit a cigarette and followed him to the car, taking in the glorious weather, eighty-five degrees and sunny in March. Instant summer! He was in a long-sleeved flannel shirt with jeans and work boots—utter winter. He didn't appear to notice my bralessness. Was I reading him wrong? That's where I'd screwed up in the past—I'd been too intense and analytic. This time, if he wasn't into it, *c'est la vie*. It was a free ticket and I had plenty of friends I could stay with. What did I have to lose that I hadn't lost already?

"You hungry?" he asked. "There's a bagel shop on the way. We'll get some. And lox," he said. "I might have to work this weekend."

"I can't wait to swim in the pool on your roof."

"I never tried it," he said, throwing my bag into the trunk of his silver Toyota Corolla. Squeezing in the driver's seat, he sloped forward, his head touching the car's roof. It was a car for someone five feet ten, not six feet four, as if he had to be physically, as well as psychically, uncomfortable in Los Angeles.

I stubbed out my cigarette. "This car's too small for you," I laughed, getting in.

"A rental. Just till the end of the season," he said. "We don't know how things are going to work out."

Was he talking about his job or our relationship? I turned on the radio to Natalie Merchant's "Cowboy Romance," opening the window. The wind blew softly through my hair. I felt lighter, tense urbanite turning into California babe. I missed guys with cars. I pictured David's silver Camaro, how we sped down Woodward

Avenue when I was fifteen, his hand on my thigh and my heart racing. I recalled soaring up the FDR Drive in Brad's blue Mazda, looking up to catch the string of lights along the Manhattan Bridge. Aaron drove slower than both of them, like an eighty-year-old geezer in Boca Raton. But I liked being driven by him.

"Tell me about your roommate, Frank," I said. "He's writing for *The Simpsons*?"

"His wife is in New York. He went back for the weekend." He turned the music down. "Frank was worried people in the building thought we were gay. I said, 'Two forty-three-year-old guys sharing a condo in Westwood. No, they think we're straight.' "

"I'll be your beard." I put my hand on his thigh. "Frank and his wife are bicoastal, good way to do it."

"He says the commute is hell," Aaron said. "This is the best job I ever had, I can't risk it."

I removed my hand.

He pointed out the best comic book emporium and the only newsstand that carried both *The New York Times* and the *New York Post*, which came two days late and cost three dollars. After we stopped at New York Bagel, he showed me his favorite used-book store.

"I heard Seinfeld's joke book is on the best-seller list out here," I said.

"Yeah. In L.A. they think it's a novel."

When we arrived, I gave myself a tour of his two-bedroom apartment. It was airy and neat, the opposite of his dim third-floor walk-up in Murray Hill, where he'd slept on a single mattress on the floor. There was room for a woman here.

"Frank found the apartment when we worked on *In Living Color*," he explained. "Furnished; a maid comes twice a week." He showed me the sunken living room, wraparound terrace, and two bathrooms. It must have been twenty-five hundred square feet.

"This would be a million dollars in Manhattan." Even the bathrooms were huge and had windows.

"It's sixteen hundred dollars a month. We split it," he said. I could split that with him, I calculated, as he led me to the bedroom. He had the biggest bed I'd ever seen.

"California king," he said. "Only thing I like out here."

Had he slept with other women on it? I noticed the Polaroid of me, which I'd express mailed, tacked to his bulletin board. He wouldn't bring another woman into a room where my picture was up. Unless he'd put it up that morning. I awkwardly unpacked. He made room in the closet. I hung up my black sundress, shirt, and pair of black jeans.

"Paying a shiva call while you're out here?" he asked.

Had he just noticed that I wore black clothes? They must have looked different in his closet. "My colorful personality makes up for it." I took out my notebook and put it on his desk. "I'm finishing a *Newsday* profile on the real Kramer. It's due Monday."

"My Kramer?" he asked.

"The title is 'The Real Kramer Steps Out of the Closet.' It's about how they stole his life for the TV character. 'Kramer looks like me, has my idiosyncrasies, and answers to my name, but I'm not right for the part,' he told me. Isn't that a great line?"

"Out of all the subjects in the world, do you have to write about Kramer?" He went to the window and opened it wide. You could hear skateboards whizzing by and lawn mowers.

I put my blow dryer and curling iron on his bathroom counter. "Well, they could have hired him for something."

Aaron took my eyelash curler from the bag. "What's this?"

"For castration," I said.

"Just what I was thinking." He squeezed it up and brought it down slowly, like it was a miniature guillotine.

"It's an assignment." Embarrassed when I came to my slinky

black teddy, I slipped it into Aaron's top drawer. Since when was I shy?

"Can't you turn it down?" He eyed the lingerie but didn't say anything.

"I already said yes. Kramer's going on *20/20* next month, so everyone will be writing about him," I said, stuffing in the rest of my underwear and bras.

"And you're just following the pack?"

"You get to write about him but I can't?"

"I'm writing lines for a character who plays Kramer," he explained.

"And I'm doing a cover story for *Newsday*'s feature section. My work isn't as important as yours?"

"I didn't say that," he said.

"You can't dictate what I write about, that's chauvinistic." After Richard I should have known to avoid older writers, they were too controlling. "I bet nobody reads *Newsday* out here anyway."

"It's owned by the same company that publishes the *L.A. Times*; they might pick it up." He readjusted my picture on the bulletin board and put another tack on the top. "They have all the New York papers flown in."

"I'm tired. Let's take a nap." I took off my black cowboy boots and socks. I'd been there an hour and my visit was already a disaster. We'd never had sex before and arguing about our conflict of interest was not an aphrodisiac. We fell asleep in our clothes far away from each other. There was a downside to such a huge bed. Hours later, I woke up wrapped in his arms.

"I don't want to fight," he said, kissing my neck.

Finally in the position for something to happen, I didn't want it to. "Let's go to the pool!" I jumped up and looked for my bathing suit.

"Too late. It closes at six."

"What about the hot tub? Come on." I went to the bathroom and changed into a black bikini. (I was in thin mode.) I wore a denim shirt over it. (Not that thin.) He went to the bathroom and came out in flowered trunks with a button-down green shirt and sneakers. He looked self-conscious and worried and cute.

"I can't believe you haven't checked out your own pool. Let's go. Do you have towels?" I found two in the linen closet.

It was cold on the roof. I stared at the foggy skyline, the sun going down. It reminded me of watching the sunset with George on the beach in Jamaica. What an elegant fish George was, swimming in the ocean so fast I couldn't keep up.

"I hate swimming," Aaron said, turning on the hot tub. The water foamed. We got in and I sidled up to him. He put his arm around me and we kissed.

"I'm glad you're here," he said. I dunked under, slipping off my bathing suit and putting his left hand on my right breast.

"You're going to get me kicked out of the building," he said, glancing nervously at the elevator.

"Stop worrying," I cooed.

We splashed and laughed and made out as the hot water swirled around us. I shut my eyes. I'd never been in a hot tub before. It was better than floating in the Caribbean, steam heating my face and shoulders. I felt far away from myself, adventurous and wild again. I didn't know you could actually do it underwater. But I got on top of him, swaying back and forth at a nice angle, surprising myself by coming quickly. Aaron pushed me in and out slowly, rubbing my back, the foamy water bubbling. "I think I love you," I whispered and he let out a moan. Previous boyfriends got off on "Fuck me harder, Tarzan," Aaron came when I said "love."

"Mr. Levin?" A short Latino man called out. Aaron jumped up, throwing me off of him. "That you? Is everything okay?" We could see a shadow walk toward us.

He pushed my head down. "Just me, Carlos. You can go. Everything's fine. Thanks." Aaron waved. *"Buenos noches."*

"Okay. Bye-bye," Carlos said, getting back in the elevator.

"We've been going out two weeks and you're already trying to drown me." I put my bathing suit back on and grabbed a towel.

"Hey." He pulled me back and wrapped his big arms around me. "Me too."

Downstairs we dried off and ordered in Chinese. Aaron put on a robe. I put on his green shirt, which was roomy and smelled like him. I could get to like it here. When the food was delivered, we took it to the living room and unpacked the cartons.

"Carlos works for the building. I'm sure everyone's already heard," Aaron said. We sat on the floor, eating with our fingers. "How could you live in New York and never have had moo shu?" He made me a pancake.

When the phone rang, he didn't move to get it. He screened his calls, viewing each one as an intrusion.

"Hi Sue! Are you here? I'm dying to see you. It's Jordan. Call me." He glared at me, horrified.

"That's my old Michigan friend Amy. I gave her your number."

"Amy? She said Jordan."

"Stage name. She does commercials. I'll see her Monday, when you're at work."

"I thought you were leaving Sunday," he said.

"I was thinking, Amy's here and my friend Tom, who I haven't seen in years. His wife hates me but maybe I can catch him at the office for lunch. And Claire's aunt is in Bel Air. I can switch the ticket and stay longer. If you don't mind." I took a bite of moo shu, gauging his reaction, dripping brown sauce down his shirt.

"In half a day you've ruined my job, my reputation in this town, and my favorite shirt." He shook his head, wet a napkin, and wiped the stain.

"I'll stay with you over the weekend, then I'll go to my friends'."
He took a shrimp dumpling. "How long will you be here?" He
popped it in his mouth and looked at me. "Exactly?"

"If I finish my profile, a few weeks. Can you loan me your fax
and typewriter?" Aaron and I were the only writers I knew who
still used typewriters, IBM Selectric IIIs, virtually impossible to
service. We talked about starting a Selectric III support group.

"You want to write a piece on my typewriter that'll get me
fired?"

"Stop being paranoid."

"That's what you told me in the hot tub."

"Are you complaining?" I took another bite of moo shu.

"Good, huh?" He made himself a bigger pancake.

"Amy can pick me up Sunday night," I said.

"Play with your friends during the day. I'm taking you to dinner
every night and you're sleeping here. With me."

This kind of chauvinism I liked. He took an extra key from his
shirt pocket and dropped it into mine. Thus we tricked our fears,
falling for each other three thousand miles from home.

19

After a whirlwind year of Aaron's commuting, his California contract wasn't renewed. He moved back east to take a job on the Jon Stewart show. Like all good comedy writers, he was bitter and depressed. Now that we were in the same city, the romance part was over, though we kept dating.

"He's working all the time. He only wants to see me Saturday nights," I complained to Dr. G. "It's boring."

"Boring is good," she said.

She was wearing a light blue dress with high heels; she was the pastel type. When I'd asked about her marital status, I'd expected her to say, "Why do you ask?" Instead, she told me she'd married young, divorced, focused on her career, and didn't remarry until forty. She had her son at forty-four. Her résumé seemed perfect, as if she'd tried to be my mother, failed, and wound up closer to me.

"How is boring good?" I asked. "Because it's not melodramatic this time?"

"He's not dazzling you with a facade or making promises he can't keep," she told me. "It's real."

"Real is defined by how unhealthy it's not?" I asked. "Why did the sex seem hotter with David, Brad, and George?"

"Because they were having hot sex with other women at the same time," she said. "While you were fantasizing about strangers."

That was the downside of arguing with someone you'd spent a dozen years spilling your guts to. "None of my other relationships were this slow."

"None of your other relationships lasted," she reminded me.

"Love is supposed to make you happy," I said.

"No it's not. Make yourself happy," she said. "A mate doesn't give you a life, they enhance the one you have."

"The fact that he won't see me more has to be a bad sign," I argued.

"I've seen men move in in three weeks. They move out just as fast," she argued back. "At least he's working his fears out now."

"You were the one who said timing was important." I'd caught her now, it was one of her mantras. "Our timing is off. I'm ready and he's not."

"It's easy to be ready with someone who isn't," was her response. "You're blaming him for boredom in your life. If you weighed 123 and were making millions writing magazine cover stories, how would you feel?"

"You're saying every single thing I've always thought about love is wrong?"

"Basically." She nodded, pointing to the clock.

When I came home from arguing with the Greenwich Village version of my mother, there was a message from the original one. "There's news. Call me right away," she said, sounding grim. Thinking someone had died, I called Mom back fast. It seemed that while I'd been gallivanting between coasts, getting shrunk, and closing in on the concept of making a living, my brothers Brian and Eric had both announced they were getting married in the fall.

Born seventeen months apart and ridiculously competitive, they fought about who was going to beat whom down the aisle. Since they'd been together three years and thus had seniority, Eric and his fiancée, Jill, decided they were taking their vows first. They were doing it in Ann Arbor, the first week of November. Then Brian and Monica, who'd been a duo only three months, planned a small wedding in Scarsdale, New York, where her mother lived, for the following weekend in November. Two brothers' weddings two weekends in a row; the thought floored me.

As the oldest and the only girl, I should have been getting hitched first. My brothers were ruining the natural order. I was beside myself. My mother was worse. For years she'd been hounding us to be normal and get married. Now that two of her kids were taking her advice, she was devastated.

"It's too quick," she said. "How can you plan weddings that quickly?"

Worse than losing her two boys, the premier party planner of West Bloomfield had not been asked to plan anything.

"I've always wanted to visit Ann Arbor," Aaron said, offering to be my date for Eric and Jill's wedding weekend. At least he was stepping up to the plate for something. "It'll be romantic."

From the moment we landed in Michigan, everything went wrong. The plane sat on the runway two hours before they found a gate. It took another hour to get our luggage, which Aaron had insisted we check. It was thirty degrees colder than in New York. I trembled in my little leather jacket as we waited for a cab to take us to the Bell Tower Hotel, where the wedding party was staying. I hated Michigan in the winter.

When we checked into our tiny room at the inn, the heat wasn't working and the bells from the clock tower across the street kept ringing in my ears. That's why they'd called it the Bell Tower; I'd just figured it out. As I was adjusting the water pressure in the shower, the shower head broke off and hit me in the head. I screwed it back on, realizing I'd forgotten hair conditioner.

"Did you bring conditioner?" I called to Aaron.

"Sorry," he called back.

"What kind of a hotel doesn't have little bottles of conditioner?" I shouted as the hot water ran out. There were only hand towels on the shelf, so I dried myself with four of them. When I put on my black hose, my nail caused a run.

"You look great," Aaron said as I sat on the green bedspread, stemming the run near my thigh with nail polish while hand-drying my tangled hair. He sat on the chair in his blue suit, reading a paperback thriller, with no idea I was about to hyperventilate.

"I'm going to find my mother." I put on my black dress and heels, grabbed my purse, and wobbled out. "Meet me downstairs."

I found her in the lobby. She was wearing a cream-colored dress with matching hose and handbag. She was in a mood herself.

"Everyone's late," she said, kissing me. "Are you okay?"

"Cool outfit." I fingered her collar. "Are we feeling neurotic or psychotic?"

"Both. We're taking pictures across the street." She pointed.

"Why can't we take them here? It's freezing out."

"Why? I don't know why," she said. "I didn't plan a family wedding dinner in Ann Arbor in November. I wasn't asked to plan anything."

Poor Mom, she wasn't even asked to bring centerpieces. Bad enough she was losing two of her sons two weeks in a row, and her only daughter was "freelance everything."

Aaron got off the elevator and joined us in the lobby. "Mrs. Shapiro, so great to meet you." He put out his hand to shake, but they wound up hugging.

My father, coming down the stairs in a black tux, found us.

"Dr. Shapiro," Aaron said, as they shook hands. "Good to be here. I always wanted to see where Sue went to school."

"The People's Republic of Ann Arbor," my father said. "I liked your *Seinfeld* show about the proctologist."

My youngest brother, Michael, showed up, in a rented tux too small for him.

"Are we having fun yet?" I asked.

"I'd rather be giving an enema," Michael said.

Eric was the first of us to get married; we were all traumatized. I thought we'd wind up like the four siblings in *The Accidental Tourist*, who grew old and demented together in their childhood home. It felt like another breakup! Eric was severing the secret sibling code. If someone was going to screw it up, it should have been me.

"Dr. Shapiro, I presume," Aaron said to Michael.

"I liked your show about the proctologist."

"His show about the marine biologist was better," I interrupted, but it was too late.

"I know a colorectal surgeon who tells me stories," Michael said. "What's a colonoscope?"

"A long tube with an asshole at either end," Aaron answered. He usually hated talking about the show he wasn't rehired on, but he was a sucker for medical malfunctions.

Monica and Brian ran in late. As if sensing a new partner in scatological humor, Brian shook Aaron's hand and said, "I have a proctologist friend who taped your show and plays it at parties."

"Figures you all like that one," I said.

"I was going to get those 'ASSMAN' license plates," said Brian.

"Someone has them. That was our inspiration. We saw 'ASSMAN' plates and guessed they belonged to a proctologist," Aaron explained. "So what's the worst thing . . ."

"A toothbrush," Michael jumped in. "It showed up on the X ray."

The men walked across the street to the room where pictures were being taken, bonding over objects people got stuck up their asses.

I walked with my mother, who was muttering about not being asked to bring the centerpieces or candy. Monica followed, in her red dress and fur coat that looked like mink. Since when had Monica, former New York intellectual, worn mink? My mother wore mink. In my absence, they'd become twins! Everything was out of whack.

"Everyone's late! Where is everyone?" Jill, the bride, yelled when we walked into the room where the photographer was snapping away. "They shot my family, now they want the men." She was a petite redhead with a bellow like Brian's.

"Is the judge here yet?" my mother said, rushing ahead. Though Jill was born Lutheran, they'd chosen a Jewish judge, as if the religion of a justice of the peace had anything to do with anything. We wanted one on our side? "Where are the men? Where's Eric?"

The women were insane, the men were serene. Odd that it was the women who'd wanted to get married.

"I'd shoot her family too," Monica said. "Can you believe the fleabag hotel? What's wrong with your hair?"

"I forgot conditioner. Stupid hotel has no heat, hot water, or conditioner. The bells are making me crazy. Isn't there a poem with bells, bells, bells, bells, bells?" I cried, running to the bathroom. It was my mother's fault: the family was too close, everyone's guts and hearts and needs overlapping. Mascara ran down my face. My nose was red. Monica stood behind me in the mirror. She was tall, big shouldered, with dark hair and outlook. With girlfriends, I gravitated toward clones. I feared that my brothers had gravitated toward stubborn, difficult women, like me.

"Boy, are you a mess," Monica laughed, took out a Kleenex, and wiped off my makeup. "Two kid brothers getting married. That's a tough one," she said. She took the brush from my purse and untangled the back of my hair. "I hated when my sister got married. I felt so alone."

"Me too," I sniffled.

"Aaron's such a big handsome guy. He fits right in," she said. "You're next."

"*You're* next!" I said. "I can't believe I have to do this again next week."

"Things went pretty well last night," Aaron said as we walked the quaint collegiate streets of Ann Arbor on Sunday.

"It was psychotic."

"At least it was small." He took my hand. "How was it psychotic?"

"Mom was upset they didn't let her plan it. Dad missed the vows 'cause he was on his cell phone with the brain hemorrhage guy. Michael and I flipped out that we're not married," I said. "You were the only one who was calm because it wasn't your family."

"Your father had an emergency," he said. "Someone was sick."

"Someone's always sick." I let go of his hand.

I didn't want to be stuck at my alma mater fifteen years later, I didn't want my brothers to be married, and I didn't want to be with a guy who couldn't even commit to living in sin. Eric and Jill had left for their honeymoon in Hawaii while Aaron and I had two hours to kill in the bleak Midwest. We strolled my old haunts, which mocked me at every turn. The reedy freshman girls wore skintight Levi's like I used to. The art movie theater had become a Limited clothing store. At Borders Books, I saw three books by classmates. Their back covers said two were professors and all three were married with children. They'd managed to publish and procreate. I'd graduated two years early but suddenly felt way behind.

"You used to hang out there?" Aaron asked, as we walked through the diagonal in the middle of campus.

I recalled sobbing on the bench in front of the library on a warm eerie spring afternoon, when I found out my first lover was sleeping with my roommate.

"Great spot," Aaron said, in a chipper mood, more anxious to stomp through my former life than I was. I pointed to what used to be the offices of *Michigas*, the humor magazine that first published my poetry and parodies.

"I remember," he said. "In the bar the girls look so fine / talking of Calvin Klein."

We went to the Jug, the all-night dive where I used to chain-smoke and scrawl poems until four in the morning. They were usually about a man, a missing man in the center. We sat down in a red-cushioned booth in the corner.

"Eric and Jill looked so happy," he said. "You should be happy for them."

Since when was Aaron Mr. Wedding Bliss? He was afraid to stay over at my apartment on a weeknight. When the waitress came I ordered a diet soda. She was tall and had long hair with bangs, the way I wore it.

"I used to go to school here," I told her. "In the late seventies."

"A while ago," she said, smiling, vacant, taking the salt shaker.

Brian's wedding was harder, because it was my fault. That past summer, when my oldest brother had accepted a job as a surgeon, he came to New York to celebrate. He stayed at the Plaza Hotel, not on my couch, as if to say, "See, I'm a man now." Since he wanted to go to dinner and a Broadway show on Saturday night, I set up a double date with Aaron and me and my friend Monica. She'd recently left publishing to go to nursing school. I figured she'd appreciate a free meal and they could talk about diseases.

After dinner and *Les Misérables*, Aaron and I took a cab downtown. "Nice try," he said. "But they had no chemistry at all." I agreed. They'd barely spoken to each other. Three days later they called from the hotel. They, as in Brian and Monica.

"We did it seven times the first night," Monica shared while he was in the bathroom.

"Yuck! Too much information!" I screamed.

Then she said something way worse: "Want a new sister-in-law?"

By the end of the summer, Brian had bought her a diamond ring and shipped Monica and all her stuff to Grand Blanc, Michigan. I'd always made fun of superficial, materialistic women whose only goal in life was getting a ring on their finger. Beware of who you trash or you'll become them. I didn't need therapy to clear my head. Envy worked faster.

Now Brian and Monica were tying the knot in Scarsdale, an hour from Manhattan. On Saturday night, mirroring my state of mind, there was a rainstorm, with fallen trees and flooding on the highways. Monica's mother had planned the reception at the Scarsdale Women's Club; she was a member. Aaron again rented a car too small for him. He didn't know how to work the windshield wipers and we got lost three times. We didn't see the sign for valet parking; I was drenched by the time we walked into the white brick building. The foyer looked pink yet austere, a library designed by Laura Ashley. My mother was there, pacing.

"We've got to stop meeting like this," I said.

"Monica's not here yet. It's five forty. Fifty people are due in twenty minutes! The ceremony starts at six. I would have made it later, but nobody asks me to plan anything." My mother's hair was perfectly puffed, even in the rain. She wore a shiny green satin dress, with a slit up the side. A bit daring for the mother of the groom, as if the glitz could make up for her lack of internal elation. I checked the mirror. I looked even worse than last weekend, in the same black velvet dress, my hair damp and frizzy. Now there'd be two photo albums documenting my ruined hair.

Uncle Izzy planted one on my cheek. "When are you gonna tie the knot? You're getting old already," he said.

"How old are you?" cousin Lenny chimed in.

"Can't wait to dance at your wedding, Susie," Aunt Rosie said. "Hurry up already."

Finally Monica rushed in, wearing jeans, T-shirt, and sneakers, running up the pink-carpeted stairs to change. Her mother followed, as did mine.

I went to find the groom. Brian looked dignified in his black tuxedo, a rose in his lapel. He'd lost thirty pounds since the summer. Monica had him working out on the Stairmaster and rowing machine. I could never get Aaron to exercise with me.

"You look handsome," I said, hyper, blurting out how all the women were late or losing it.

"Don't worry, sis," he said, smiling and jovial, man of the hour. "Everyone's just nervous. Thank you for introducing us. Everything's fine."

Monica looked wonderful, walking down the makeshift aisle in a tight lacy low-cut white gown. After a short ceremony by another Jewish judge (Monica was Protestant), there was dinner and dancing. Aaron and I were seated at the head table, next to the bride and groom I'd accidentally brought together. The waiter said choice of entrée was salmon or steak. I picked neither; I'd lost my appetite. Aaron and Brian chose steak. Monica said, "Both." She was the only bride I'd ever seen eat at her own wedding, finishing the two dinners with gusto.

"You okay?" Michael asked me. "Need some Xanax?" In the same too-small tuxedo as last week, he was sweating. He looked worse than I did.

"No. Just a dance," I said, leading him to the makeshift wooden floor, where newlyweds Eric and Jill glided past us.

"I had to leave Hawaii for this pastel shit?" Jill called out to us.

"Just don't get married this year," Michael told me.

"I promise," I said, spinning the rim of my black velvet dress, feeling alone, like the last Jewess in the world, only the sister.

Brian and Monica were staying at a Scarsdale hotel, then leaving for their two-week honeymoon in Belize early the next morning. I was jealous and fuming as Aaron drove us home at five miles an hour in the rainstorm. My two kid brothers could get married. Even my friend Monica could do it. Why the hell couldn't I ever close the deal?

At my apartment, I dried off, changing from my black dress into black sweats and a T-shirt. I put the three rose centerpieces I'd sneaked out with into a vase; at least I got pretty flowers out of the deal. Aaron took off his tux jacket and undid his bow tie. The storm died down and it was drizzling outside.

"What a nice party. It went really well, I thought." Aaron sat down next to me and rubbed my neck.

"I've been dating since I was thirteen," I said. "I'm sick of boyfriends. I want a husband."

He stopped rubbing. "I'm tired. Want to crash?"

"No. I want to talk," I said.

"Not again." He took off his shoes, revealing a hole in his sock. "I've been really depressed and you keep insisting . . ."

"You've been depressed for months," I said. "You can be depressed and married."

"I don't want to get married. I'm not ready to live together, and I don't want children," he said.

I looked at Aaron, with his wet, wilty mop of hair and fat, ugly toes.

"Go home," I said.

20

I hadn't spoken to Aaron in three months. My two married brothers announced that their wives were pregnant in time for my thirty-fifth birthday. Since panic and desperation were good motivators, I lost twelve pounds, bought miniskirts and Wonderbras, and begged friends to fix me up. I'd set up seven marriages for other people, Brian and Monica unwittingly. The reciprocal God of fix-ups owed me big.

My first blind date was with Joshua Stone, a thirty-five-year-old Episcopalian psychoanalyst from Pennsylvania who was getting divorced. When I met him for a drink at Greenwich Café, I was pleased to find that Joshua was tall, thin, and boyishly handsome. He wore jeans with a tweed jacket I liked, and ordered Pinot Grigio, tasting it and nodding to the waiter. He seemed urbane and sophisticated—until he opened his mouth.

"I love Manhattan. I grew up here. We used to come here, my wife, Deborah, and I. Well, soon-to-be-ex-wife, I should say. She hated New York. I shouldn't talk about her." He spoke faster than I did. "I haven't been in the dating scene long. I never was, unless you count high school. Though I didn't get laid in high school. Deborah was my first." He looked at the floor. "I shouldn't have told you that, I just . . ."

"It's okay, I like neurotics," I said. "Especially one going through an emotional crisis."

"Is that your diagnosis?" He laughed, a long easy laugh. "I thought I was the fastest diagnostician in the East. I have competition."

I crossed my legs, self-conscious in my short skirt and low-cut sweater, more comfortable playing shrink than siren. "Let's hear the Deborah story."

"We met at Harvard when I was nineteen. We were in the psych program. After dating for six months, I proposed . . ."

"Why so young?"

"I was stupid." He looked at the menu. "Let's eat. How's the grilled vegetables?"

"What was your home like when you grew up?"

"Another Freudian. My father left when I was three. My mother was a workaholic who founded a feminist magazine."

"Aha!" I said. "You needed instant family."

"Right." He ordered a fruit platter. A health nut. I hated health nuts. "We had two little girls, moved to the burbs. Deborah gave up her practice and hounded me to make more money. I was earning two hundred thousand a year, but that wasn't enough. She stayed home all day, started calling herself Debbie. Total regression, my worst nightmare . . ."

"You wanted a Deborah but she turned into a Debbie?" I asked. He nodded. "But you didn't want a real mommy type. You wanted a career mommy, like the one you had."

"Well, everything was fine until she stopped sleeping with me. For two years, nothing. Unless you count with myself. Then I met Arlene, who was hot, but she dumped me. Am I telling you too much?"

"Might as well get the psychosexual history out of the way." I laughed again and pulled out a cigarette. Joshua lit it, then took out one of his own. A man who smoked, what a relief. He was pretty raw, but I was enjoying his ramble. It made me feel like I was stable.

"You just split with someone too," he said. "What happened?"

"Comedy writer paralyzed by depression."

"He couldn't commit?" Joshua looked at me sympathetically; he was the doctor now. He seemed too nuts to be seeing patients, but he was empathetic.

I nodded. "And my two younger brothers just got married. A week apart."

"Double family wedding trauma?" Josh asked.

"Right. Aaron came with me to both weddings, but he's forty-five years old and . . ."

"Never been married?"

"Never."

"You only like me because I'm the opposite of Aaron," he said. When our salad and fruit plate arrived, he asked for a side order of fries. Fries and cigarettes—there was hope.

"How do you know I like you?"

"I made you laugh twice," he said.

I crossed my legs back and pulled my sweater up, wishing I wasn't wearing the Wonderbra. It was too tight, pushing my breasts together. What was the point of a contraption that made me look bigger to land a guy? What about seduction? Wouldn't he be aghast to discover he'd picked up Dolly Parton but woke up next to Gloria Steinem? Luckily Joshua didn't notice anything but the food. He wolfed down the apples and melon, and picked at my salad. I finished the wine, feeling light-headed.

"What if I'm the anti-Deborah and your mother rolled into one?" I stole a slice of mango from his plate. "Could be dangerous."

"Not if you're on rebound," he said.

"You're on double rebound and you're only interested in me because I'm not really available," I countered.

"Good point." He finished the wine, ordered a second bottle, and lit another cigarette. "What are you doing tomorrow night?" he asked. "Want to go out again?"

"Boy, you're green."

"You're an expert at this?"

"Yes. I have six failed relationships on my résumé. One more ridiculous than the next. Though you're my first date since Aaron and I split up."

"You're the second woman I've liked since Deborah threw me out. Arlene was the first. She's a psychologist in my office. We spent a wild two weeks in bed and . . ."

"Okay," I interrupted. "I'm teaching you how to date. Lesson number one, keep your salary and sex life to yourself. Lesson number two, don't ask for a second date until you've finished the first."

"Why? I'm only in town for four days and . . ."

"Because you look insecure and hard up."

"I *am* insecure and hard up," he said. When the fries came, he splashed on ketchup and scarfed them down. I never saw anyone eat so fast, as fast as he talked.

"Listen," I said, "seems like you should screw around a lot. Sleep with twenty or thirty women, get it out of your system."

"I'm already hypomanic!" he said. "Why won't you go out with me again?"

"You're not even legally separated and you live in Pennsylvania."

"If the woman I loved lived in New York, I'd move to New York."

"That's a good thing to decide on a first date."

"Does that mean you won't go out with me tomorrow night?" He cracked up again.

At my apartment, I sat on the couch and Joshua sat a cushion away. He'd come on so strong but he already needed space.

"Want to get high?" He looked younger in the bright light, like he was nineteen. If they'd been in the same room, you'd think Aaron was his father. Food, cigarettes, wine, dope, talking nonstop—

it was fascinating to watch someone with a worse oral fixation than mine. He pulled rolling papers from his wallet, which was over-stuffed. He was the type to keep a bunch of pictures in there.

"Let me see your photos," I said.

"This is Arlene."

"I don't want to see a picture of your lover."

"Okay. Sorry." He put Arlene back and pulled out Deborah.

"Your ex-wife?" How dumb was this guy? "You want to show me pictures of your prom date?"

He took out pictures of his two daughters. Professionally taken against a blue background, a little too posed. He put them down on the couch and rolled a joint.

"You put your daughters between us," I said.

He looked at the photos beside him, then at me. "You're out-shrinking me," he said, taking off his shoes. He went to the CD player and pulled out an oldies compilation.

"This is the best tune," he said as "Do You Love Me?" came on. I hated that jumpy, juvenile song. He danced around the living room, singing "Do you love me—now that I can dance?" I joined him and we bopped around, passing the joint back and forth.

"Can I read your work? Are you as funny on paper?" He turned the CD to the same song and danced to it again in a cloud of smoke, by himself. "We used to dance to this in college."

I pulled out a few humor pieces, put them in an envelope.

"Dance with me again," he said.

"I'm throwing you out." I pointed to my watch. "It's four in the morning."

"Really? I can't stay?"

I turned off the music and handed him his shoes. I kissed Joshua on the cheek, gave him the envelope with my clips, and literally pushed him out the door. Ten minutes later, the phone rang.

"This piece on committing to a one-night stand is hilarious," he said. "I can't stop laughing."

"Where are you?"

"Phone booth on Seventeenth Street and Eighth Avenue," he said. "Will you have dinner with me tomorrow night? Please?"

"Rule number three," I said. "Never say please."

I made out with Joshua in New York three weekends in a row but wouldn't sleep with him. Then I flew to Michigan for my birthday. Joshua shocked me on Saturday by pulling up my parents' driveway in a yellow convertible. He'd driven ten hours to surprise me! He was bearing flowers, candy, and Motown CDs. I felt like a teenager when a new suitor came calling. My mother was as charmed as I was. My father wasn't. Dad obnoxiously gave Joshua his left hand to shake and asked why he had never gone to medical school to become a real physician.

Brian and Eric and their pregnant wives came over to celebrate my birthday. Eric drilled Joshua on the reasons for his divorce (he and his wife hated each other) and when it would be final (next year). Upping the Shapiro male rudeness factor, Brian asked if Joshua was worried that his two kids would be permanently damaged by his divorce.

"He seems wound up," Monica whispered. "What is he? Hypomanic?"

I was annoyed that she'd diagnosed Joshua accurately. She really had joined the family.

Michael had the weekend off; he'd driven in from Chicago. He laughed loudly at Joshua's joke about how to run an Episcopalian out of town ("Burn a question mark on their front lawn"). But then Michael pulled me aside and said, "We miss Aaron."

"Then you marry him," I said.

Back in New York, since I was seriously contemplating sleeping with someone else, Aaron's male radar went into overdrive. He had left two messages. "Hi. How's it going? I wanted to say hi," one said. I erased it. His next message was equally lame. "Wanted to say happy birthday. Hope you're well." I zapped that one too. While I was unpacking, the doorman buzzed to say, "Mr. Aaron is here. Should I send him up?"

"Sure." It was good timing. I was wearing my twenty-eight-inch-waist Levi's, which fit again. In all my years of erotic field research and clinical testing, there was only one thing I'd learned for sure about the male species: nothing worked faster than the scent of another man.

I opened the door and stared at him.

"Hi," Aaron said. "Where've you been?" His jeans were ripped at the knee and he hadn't shaved, an obvious ploy for sympathy.

"Michigan."

"How's your family?" He sat down on the couch, flipped through a *New Yorker* on the coffee table.

"Monica and Jill are pregnant."

"More Christopher Buckley crap on the back page," he said.

"He should stick to sailing," I agreed.

"What's new?" he asked.

"I'm seeing someone new."

"A new shrink?" he asked.

"Well, he's a shrink," I said. "He's also single. His name is Joshua."

"You're dating a shrink?" Aaron was flabbergasted.

"You dated a shrink," I said. "He's sort of single. Going through a divorce."

"Divorce. Bad sign." Aaron spoke more slowly than Joshua, his words more deliberate. His manner was older, he knew who he was. Yet that meant he couldn't change. Men my age were more malleable.

"Eighty percent of divorced men remarry in seventeen months," I said.

"Is *Cosmo* your bible?" he asked.

"I used to write for *Cosmo*."

"How long have you known him?"

"Three months," I said. "But he wants to remarry and . . ."

"He mentions marriage after two weeks and you didn't run in the other direction?"

"Some men are fast. My brother Brian proposed in three months."

"If Brian is so great, why don't you marry him?"

"Freud would say I did; he married my girlfriend."

"You just like Joshua because he's the opposite of me."

Joshua thought I liked him because he was the opposite of Aaron. It was a new form of male egotism. "Exactly," I said. "He drove all the way to Michigan to see me."

"He was in Michigan with you? He met your family?" Aaron put down the magazine. He looked crushed, as he was supposed to.

No more Ms. Nice Guy for me.

"He stayed in a hotel," I added. I wasn't a total shrew. I was about to tell Aaron that my father and brothers had voted for him, but stopped myself.

"Is this serious?"

"It's nice being with a guy who doesn't need ten years to figure it out."

"I don't need ten years," Aaron said. "I just need a little more time."

Aha! A time frame. This was a new development.

"How much time?"

"Six months."

"Too long." I sat down on the couch and picked up the magazine, paging through, stopping at a searing, confessional poem I liked by Louise Gluck. "At least Tina Brown didn't fuck with *The New Yorker*'s poetry," I said.

"Three months," he said. "But stop seeing him."

"Six weeks," I said. "And I see who I want."

* * *

I kept seeing Joshua when he came to New York. But I wasn't ready to sleep with him, meet his daughters, or visit Pennsylvania (I barely made it above Fourteenth Street).

When Aaron stopped by six weeks later, I was sure he'd ask for another week or month or year and try to seduce me. Yet this time he walked in, put his hand in his briefcase, and pulled out a red velvet heart-shaped box. He knelt down in front of me and almost fell over. I helped him straighten up. He opened it and showed me a diamond ring on a platinum band.

"Want to get married?" he asked.

"Yes," I said, too quickly.

He sat on the couch and looked at me, as if he didn't know what was supposed to happen next. I didn't know either. I was way better prepared for a breakup than for a proposal. Breakups were easy. When a guy dumped me, I cried, got drunk, called all my girlfriends, and immediately went back on the prowl to spite him. What to do after a proposal was accepted had never occurred to me. I kissed Aaron, played with his hair. Maybe you were supposed to have sex, but I just wanted to call my mother.

"I bought the ring ten days ago," he said. "Every morning I'd look at it. Part of me wanted to give it to you earlier. The other part hoped it had disappeared during the night."

"It's beautiful," I said, staring at the box he was still holding.

"Can we order in moo shu?" he asked.

"You have to put the ring on me first."

But he couldn't; the ring was too tight. I was afraid to mar the mood. I was afraid he'd change his mind. I was afraid he'd see that his betrothed had fat fingers. I ran to the bathroom, used soap to get it on. I ignored the swelling and red patches that formed around my finger. Before we went to bed, I had to sneak to the bathroom to secretly scrape soap against the back to get it off.

Two minutes after Aaron left on Sunday morning, I called my mother. "Mom, I have news. I'm getting married!" I shouted. "He proposed."

"Who?" my mother asked.

"Aaron."

"What did you say?" She sounded very calm.

"What do you mean what did I say? I said yes!"

"Are you sure?"

"Of course I'm sure. What's wrong with you?" I yelled. "You've been telling me to get married for thirty-five years and now that I'm doing it, you ask if I'm sure?"

"I never told you to get married," she said.

"Mom, you used to walk into my room when I was playing with my Barbies and say 'No man is going to marry such a slob.' When I was four years old."

"That's not telling you to get married. That's telling you to clean up your room," she said. "Jack, pick up the phone. Your daughter has news."

"What?" my father said.

"I'm getting married!" I told him.

"To who?" my father asked.

The next call I made was to Joshua. At least he wouldn't ask who the groom was.

"I knew it!" Joshua said. "Aaron got jealous. Your relationship wasn't over."

"I'm sorry," I said. "I thought it was."

"I got you married," Joshua said. "I'm your marriage fluffer."

"That's good. Can I steal that?" I asked. "And I'm not married yet."

"That's true. Can we still talk?" he asked.

"Sure," I said. "What's up?"

On the phone for two hours, our relationship somehow transformed into friendship. He admitted that Arlene had been calling and that he had met a cute French social worker in the next office. "Ask her to lunch," I said. "Don't mention marriage until date ten."

A day later an envelope arrived, containing three joints and six humor pieces Joshua had written, with me in the female lead. I faxed him back my comments with stars on the good lines. He faxed me a note that said, "Can I be your second husband?"

The next time Aaron came over, he decided to call my parents and tell them himself. "Are you up for another wedding?" he asked my mother. While they were talking, the doorman buzzed. I went to the intercom to answer it, wrong buzzer. When I returned I heard Aaron say, "Sure. For our wedding, anything you want."

I shook my head, flailed my arms, mouthed the word *No!*, and did a "time-out" sign. Too late. Ten minutes after he hung up, the rabbi called. Then the cantor. The caterer. The florist. The bandleader. To my mother, "anything you want" turned out to be plans for a black-tie sit-down dinner in August, at a Bloomfield Hills country club with chuppah, rabbi, four courses, six musicians, and me in a long white gown. There was only one problem. I'd already decided to wear black to a loud, funky, late-night dance party for our friends at a loft in Soho, where we'd be married in a casual civil ceremony.

I booked an emergency last-minute double appointment with Dr. G. I didn't want to hurt my mother, but I had a right to plan my own wedding. Dr. G. and I decided that if my brothers could wed two weekends in a row, so could we. The black wedding, with a civil ceremony, would be in my city. The white wedding, with rabbi and cantor, would be in my mother's.

When we asked Aaron's father, a judge, to marry us at the first wedding, Aaron's parents were thrilled. Since late-night SoHo cocktail parties were relatively low rent, my parents offered to pay—as long as we did the white wedding their way. I went from never getting married to doing it twice!

"Your brothers did it two weekends in a row; you're just being competitive," Aaron said.

I soon heard myself talking about bridal dresses, bridal showers, and bridal registries. Where did this bridal stuff come from? I never wanted to be a bride, I hated brides. As a kid I'd colored Barbie's white wedding ensemble black with Flair pens.

"I can't stand women who obsess about weddings," I cried to Dr. G. "How can you become your worst fear?"

"Patty Hearst went from SLA guerrilla to housewife," she offered.

"She was kidnapped!" I yelled.

"What are you afraid of?"

I paraphrased a poem I recalled about an evil witch in a nightmare, who shows up screaming, "You are ordinary. You are ordinary. You are ordinary."

"Getting married means you're ordinary?"

"Conventional," I said. "Maybe that's why I'm having two weddings. But I'm afraid I'm doing both of them for the wrong reasons."

"What are the wrong reasons?"

"If my brothers can do it, I can too," I counted off. "I'll never find anyone taller . . . If I die tomorrow, I'd rather my obit said I was divorced than never married. Isn't that horrible?"

"Whatever gets you there." She shrugged. "What are the right reasons?"

"Mad, passionate love."

"That's infatuation. It hardly ever lasts."

"Kids. Kids last . . . We haven't even approached the subject of kids."

"Why don't we wait awhile on that one?" she said, smiling.

"I'm inviting you to the wedding," I warned her. "The black one."
I became scared, spacey, and confused, my mind boggled that
one could go from breakup to marriage in a matter of minutes.
Meanwhile, Aaron turned gung ho. He chatted with my mother
on the phone daily about the color of tablecloths, which appetizers
would be served, and the flavor of the wedding cake.

Suddenly an engagement ring expert, on Monday morning he
said, "First let's go get the ring sized and readjusted in a classic
Tiffany setting." The jeweler said size six was too small and suggested six and a half. I insisted on size seven so I could slip it on
and off easily. Then the jeweler asked me for the ring back for ten
days. It had taken me thirty-five years to land the most important
piece of jewelry in my life and he wanted to take it away. He caught
the look on my face and said, "Five days." I called him at 9 A.M. on
Friday. He said, "It's ready." I picked it up at 9:13.

On the way home I was acutely aware of my new piece of jewelry. I felt a surge of fear on the subway. What if I were mugged? I
imagined the *New York Post* headline—"Downtown Girl Dies for
Diamond" and I put on the fur-lined gloves my mother had given
me, to hide it. I was moving my arms differently. My left hand felt
heavier, like I was walking lopsided. At my apartment I tried on all
my clothes to see how they looked with it. Then I wore the ring
and nothing else and danced around my apartment to Gloria
Gaynor's "I Will Survive."

The ring was a little too loose and sometimes shifted to the inside of my hand without my realizing it. When I went to rub blush
on my cheeks, it scratched my face. I sat down at my Selectric, but
I couldn't write with the ring on. I took it off, put it back into its
little red velvet heart, and closed the lid fast. I left it on my desk.
With my finger bare again, the words flowed, but I felt as if somebody was spying on me. I opened up the box to glare at the suspi-
cious shining eye, which was staring back.

21

Since I refused to wear white for wedding number one, my mother did. She showed up at the SoHo loft at 8:30 P.M. in a beaded pearl gown, looking more like the bride than I did. The ceremony was at nine o'clock sharp. I was in a knee-length strapless black chiffon number I'd found for a hundred dollars at a Village boutique, and high heels I couldn't walk in. My father said "Hi, Morticia." He hated the SoHo gallery I'd chosen for the reception, five blocks from Delancey Street, where his father's window shade store used to be.

"Afraid of your ghosts?" I asked.

"If you had my ghosts you'd be afraid too," he said.

"If?"

"Look, we hung window shades right across the street." My father showed Aaron the row of long windows and pointed. "You're doing this to spite us."

"She picked the loft," Aaron pointed to me.

Aaron's father, Judge Harry Levin, who was marrying us, was in black too—his judge's robe worn over his tux. Aaron's mother, Sonya, wore a beige lace dress. She hugged me hello and said, "We're so glad he picked you. We didn't like his other girlfriends."

The first time I'd met Aaron's parents we'd hit it off so well

Aaron had said, "Now I'll never get rid of you." His father was an older version of my father, a straight shooter, medical jargon replaced by legalese, same workaholic tendencies. His mother was warm and funny and kind of an open book, like my mother. Both sets of parents, who'd just met at dinner two days before, seemed like lifelong friends. They hugged and kissed hello, bonded in the glee that their offspring were finally doing something socially respectable.

"Dr. Shapiro, we're so happy to have Susan in our family," Aaron's father said.

"Judge Levin, we couldn't be happier," my father said.

"They're going to call each other Judge and Doctor all night," Aaron said in my ear.

"Don't you think they should sign a Ketubah?" Aaron's mother asked about the traditional Jewish wedding contract.

"The rabbi can do it in Michigan next weekend," my father answered.

"Good, they need a Ketubah. The doctor is right," Aaron's father said.

"Judge, I couldn't agree more," my father said.

"We grew up in the same family," I told Aaron.

"The only son being a writer is worse than the only daughter being a writer," Aaron argued.

"Okay, you win this round, you're more screwed up than I am," I said. It was an ongoing game.

The deejay I'd hired, Mr. Music, came up the stairs. Like my mother, he was also wearing white—a white tuxedo. "Something's wrong with the elevator," he said. "My assistant can't get the equipment up."

"Maybe that's why it's nine o'clock and hardly anyone's here," said Aaron.

"I'm going downstairs to find my brother and sister," my mother said. A few minutes later she came back, rushing up the stairs, sweating, holding up the bottom of her gown. She was on the verge of hysteria. "Aunt Rosie and Uncle Izzy were trapped in the elevator for half an hour. They were scared to death. They went back to New Jersey!"

"They can take the stairs. It's only five flights," Aaron interjected. "I'll help them."

"It's too late, they left!" My mother scowled at me.

"I warned you it was an old loft building," I said. She'd promised to invite all her friends and relatives to wedding number two, the next weekend, in Michigan. But the New Jersey kin wanted to come to both—though I warned her it would be a semibizarre bash for two hundred poet-journalist-and-comedy writer friends of mine and Aaron's.

"Only you would get married at nine o'clock at night in a warehouse," she said.

"Mom, calm down."

"Don't tell me to calm down," she said. "What's wrong with the air-conditioning?"

It was a ninety-degree summer night, so of course the air-conditioner broke. The gallery owner, whom Aaron reached at a party in East Hampton, called in for big standing fans, which were delivered at ten minutes after nine, as the guests starting coming, by way of the stairs. Whoever said weddings were romantic was single and/or in the wedding business.

"What's wrong with the elevator?" Claire asked, arriving with my college pal Paul. "We waited half an hour downstairs."

"Some old people who came out of the elevator looked shook up," Paul said.

"Sorry." I hugged Claire. "Old building."

"Only you would get married in a warehouse," Paul said. I hadn't invited any old boyfriends, though I was sure Paul would tell everything to his pal Brad (heartbreak number one). I hoped he'd skip the broken elevator and the lack of air-conditioning.

The big, creaky elevator, now working again, opened with twenty people crammed in, including my brothers and sister-in-law Jill. She'd recently had a miscarriage; I was touched she still came. (Monica, eight and a half months pregnant, couldn't fly in for the occasion.) Aaron's sister, brother-in-law, and cousins spilled out, along with my shrink. Dr. G. actually showed up! She introduced her husband, Dr. K. He was a shrink too, I learned. I noted that she'd kept her own name, like I was going to do. It was the first time I'd seen her out of therapy, but she looked the same. Taller maybe, since I'd mostly seen her sitting down. Her husband was a cute teddy-bear type. No wonder she'd been rooting for Aaron; she wanted me to have what she had. She'd sent a blown-glass vase the day before, which I'd overanalyzed. It was to grow things, to display beauty in. Bright colors, except for the little specks of dark blue in the corners, as if to respect the sadness.

My L.A. friend Amy/Jordan clodded up the steps in high heels. She'd insisted on coming to both weddings too. "Hiya babydoll." She kissed me. "Far-out dress. Your mother's flipping out. Something about losing Izzy and Rosie in the elevator."

"There's the bride!" said my old college roommate Nicole. Although she'd slept with my boyfriend David (heartbreak number five) in college, we had stayed friends.

"Where's Billy?" I asked about her husband.

"I'm filing for divorce," Nicole said.

"I'm sorry," I said. "What happened?"

"I understood his mood swings and fear of failing like his father, but then he wouldn't fuck me," Nicole said. "Make sure he wants to fuck you." She went to the bar and got a drink.

Kyla, my other college pal involved in the David fiasco, came out of the next elevator with Sally, who'd dated Richard (heartbreak number four). The triangles of my life were congregating in front of me. Happily they felt more amusing than scary.

"Come on, I think we're ready," Aaron said, grabbing my arm.

He led me to the broomstick and sheet we were pretending was a chuppah in the front of the loft.

"Aaron, do you have the ring?" his father called.

"No, I forgot it, Dad." He rolled his eyes.

"Show it to me." His father persisted.

"You don't believe I remembered the ring?" Aaron laughed, but it felt like a reenactment of his life story. Our families, not subtle enough to be passive/aggressive, were aggressive/aggressive.

"Everyone, quiet. Take your seats. Quiet please." Judge Levin took control. "I've been waiting a long time to do this," he said. "Forty-six years to be exact."

"Is he trashing me at my own wedding ceremony?" Aaron asked. I laughed.

"You think this is funny?" the judge teased me. "You have to live with him."

"Just who we wanted to marry us," Aaron said. "Henny Youngman."

"We're so glad he chose you," the judge said. "We didn't like any of his other girlfriends."

"Okay, Dad," Aaron said.

"Okay. We're ready. No more laughing," he said, placing Aaron to my right. Everyone sat down on the folding chairs we'd set up in front of the chuppah. Judge Levin cleared his throat and launched into the civil ceremony. "We are gathered here tonight to join this couple in the bond of holy wedded matrimony . . ."

I stared at Aaron, who looked handsome in his tux, thanking God that I got a tall one. Did I notice a tear in his eye as he slipped the wedding ring on my finger? We smashed the glass together and kissed awkwardly in front of his father. Everyone applauded. Then a cocktail buffet was served by six waiters in black.

"You should join them," my mother said. "You're dressed for it."

"It's not my fault Izzy and Rosie got caught in the elevator," my father told my mother. "What's this?" He grabbed an hors d'oeuvre from a tray and showed it to her.

"Brie en croûte," she said. I'd let her take charge of the food, though it took months to talk her out of a six-course sit-down dinner for the black wedding. She did insist on bringing four huge baskets of candy, which—with the help of my father, brothers, and Jill—she carried on the plane.

My father put it in his mouth and mumbled, "Fancy cheese knish."

Mr. Music, who'd finally gotten his equipment and assistant up in the elevator, called Aaron and me to dance to our special wedding song: "Runaround Sue." Our friends cracked up, gathering on the wooden floor to disco-rap-bump-and-break-dance. I threw off my high heels and careened shoeless into the middle, spinning. Everything seemed gleeful as my mother and father and three brothers twirled around me. When "Stop in the Name of Love" came on, Claire and I pantomimed the movements of the Supremes.

Dr. G., who was dancing with her husband, signaled to me. I made it over to her side of the dance floor. "Thanks for the vase. It's beautiful," I told her. "And for coming. And for all you've done for me."

She pulled me close. I thought she had profound final advice to give me. But she asked, "Is there more than one Nicole?"

"No, that's my old college roommate, the one who slept with David," I answered.

"Is that the Sally who went with the dog?" She pointed to Sally, in a red dress, drunk out of her mind. She was telling the story, of me and her and Richard and Oscar, to a crowd that had gathered near the bar.

"Yes, Richard's ex ex, Oscar's mother," I said, realizing Dr. G.

was meeting years' worth of characters from my psychodramas in the flesh. "Did you meet my mom?"

"Yes. The one in white." She laughed. "But which one is your sister-in-law Monica?"

"She couldn't come. She's too pregnant to fly," I told her.

"At least she didn't have the baby on your wedding day," Dr. G. said.

The next Saturday, the day of our second wedding, I woke up in my old pink room in Michigan, my Barbie dolls glaring at me from the shelf. It was noon. My family was supposed to be at the country club for photographs at five. Where was everyone? Downstairs I found three notes on the kitchen table. The first, on my mother's ivory stationery, said: "Monica had the baby at nine this morning. Sammy Shapiro, eight pounds, four ounces. Everyone's fine! Went to see them. Back by four, honey. Mom." A page from my father's prescription pad said: "Drove to the Flint Hospital with Mike. Dad." At least Monica wouldn't give birth to the first grandchild of the family in the middle of my ceremony, as I'd bet Aaron.

On a Post-it note Aaron scrawled: "Meeting with Frank at the hotel. See you tonight. Love you madly." He and his old L.A. roommate, Frank, were writing an ABC pilot about Brooklyn surfers. He'd informed me that he and Frank were leaving for L.A. Sunday night.

"Have a nice honeymoon," I'd said.

I phoned Claire and Amy/Jordan at the hotel where they were staying, but nobody was around. Wasn't that what the bridesmaids and maids of honor were for? Perhaps I shouldn't have nixed the whole entourage thing. That was the problem with a second wedding in two weeks: nobody returned your calls. Nobody left me a car, so I couldn't even get to 7-Eleven. It was sunny, so I went out to lie by the pool in our backyard. I did the *New York Times* cross-word puzzle in pen, but I needed Aaron for the "3-time Yank MVP." I swam thirty laps without my top on. If I had to be stuck in Bloomfield by myself, I might as well be risqué. The laundry guy dropped off shirts at the side door. I hoped he saw me and got a cheap thrill.

Inside I checked my New York messages. There was only one, from a big literary agent I'd sent my work to. She said she'd loved it, I was hysterical, and we should arrange a meeting soon. I tried to call her back six times but nobody picked up. (I'd forgotten it was Saturday.) I took a shower, then pulled my white wedding gown from the closet. It was low cut and plain. Mom and I had found it, on sale and off the rack, at Saks. I put it on and looked in the mirror. Definitely not me. I felt awkward, like an actress reprising a role I'd walked out on decades ago, swearing I'd never return.

My mother, never late a day in her life, showed up at twenty minutes past five, kissing me, tucking in my bra strap. "You look so pretty in white," she said.

"This agent left a message for me in New York! She wants me to call her."

"You should have seen the baby. He's so adorable."

"Can I wear black hose with a white dress?" I asked. "It's long. Nobody'll see."

"No. You'll have black toes." She made a face. "I bought you three pairs of Givenchy hose in white."

"She works for a huge agency. I think Wendy Wasserstein is one of their clients."

My mother went to her room to get dressed. At five thirty my father's car pulled into the garage. He and my brother Michael raced upstairs to put on their tuxes. I ripped two pairs of hose with my engagement ring. Then I attempted to put on makeup and curl my hair at the same time.

"Mom!" I yelled. She rushed in, armed with her makeup bag. She brushed pink blush on my cheeks. She painted on lipstick. "Not in your eyes for once." She combed my bangs to the side.

"The agent thinks I'm hysterical."

"She doesn't have to live with you," my mother said.

Aunt Rosie, Uncle Izzy, and cousin Lenny were at the club an hour early. They'd forgiven me for the loft's defective elevator last week and had driven all the way here from New Jersey. They obviously couldn't wait to congratulate me.

"You're a grandpa now," cousin Lenny told my father, patting him on the back.

"Hello Grandma," Rosie told my mother. Rosie was in a black dress I wished I was wearing. "You're too sexy to be a grandma. Can you believe she's a grandma, Izzy?"

Aaron walked over to me. "Hey, how's it going?" he said casually, as if he'd bumped into a pal at Starbucks. He looked even taller in his black tux. But why was he carrying his briefcase?

"Gonna work between courses?" I asked, kissing him on the lips.

"You look stunning." He put his arm round me. A copy of his pilot script was in his briefcase, I was sure. It was an obsessive-compulsive disorder we shared, bringing work with us to the oddest places. I thought of how Rilke defined love, as "two solitudes that protect and border and salute each other."

"Are you nervous?" I asked him.

"Not in the least," he said. "It helps that we're already married."

"Your first grandchild!" Rosie squealed. "I can't believe you're a grandma."

"Did you hear about Monica?" I asked him.

"I win. It wasn't in the middle of the ceremony," said Aaron.

I said a silent prayer for Jill and Eric to get pregnant again.

We went out back to the gazebo to take photographs, the posed kind with the sunset in the background I swore I'd never be caught dead in. Aaron's parents showed up, looking splendid in their evening attire. They were so excited Aaron was married, they would have come to a third wedding next week.

"The baby is a Leo, like you and me," Uncle Izzy told my father.

"Eight pounds, four ounces," someone else said.

Were they giving out birth announcements at the door?

"Are you next?" cousin Lenny asked me.

"What a day!" said Rosie. "Double mazel."

Since we were already married, we'd asked Rabbi Lutz for a short, lighthearted ceremony. He'd shrugged and said, "I am what I am," and launched into an hour speech of Hebrew prayers and Talmudic wisdom about eternal love. Aaron looked enraptured, nodding as the rabbi came to "I am my beloved and my beloved is mine."

After smashing the glass a second time in two weeks, I drank five glasses of champagne and wobbled through the dining room. It was filled with fancy black tablecloths and white-rose-and-orchid centerpieces. There were two hundred people, many I didn't know. Leave it to my mother—even the men, in black tuxes and white silk yarmulkes, matched the decor. Everyone took their seats. The head table was missing my brother Brian and Monica. I knew she didn't plan to go into labor this morning, but I missed my brother. Aaron kissed me.

"This big agent in New York left a message. She thinks I'm hysterical."

"She doesn't have to live with you," he said.

Aaron's Uncle Al, who was almost blind, came up to cut the

challah bread, which he missed three times. Judge Levin, father of the groom, insisted on making a toast.

"My wife and I feel that Aaron should have made this decision a long time ago," he said, lifting his glass. "We love Susan, and I sentence them both to life—with no parole."

"Great, Dad," Aaron said. "Critique my past for a second time and then use jail imagery."

The band played their repertoire of cheesy wedding songs. Ricardo, the hairdresser, did the Macarena with Jill, Amy/Jordan and Aunt Rosie. My parents tangoed to "How High the Moon." The entire Shapiro and Levin clans got up to hora. Claire grabbed my brother Michael and led him to the dance floor. My father and I slow danced to "Sunrise, Sunset." In the middle someone tapped me on the shoulder. It was my brother Brian, in his tux. He had a huge grin on his face. He swept me around the dance floor to the sounds of clapping and flashcubes going off, as if we were the ones getting married.

"Thanks for coming," I said.

"Wouldn't miss it for the world."

"Nothing like upstaging me," I told him.

"Shut up, you're already married."

"I can't believe you're a father." I rested my head on my brother's shoulder.

He whispered, "I can't believe you're wearing white."

22

Lori wants to meet you," Aaron said.

I turned off the TV. I'd been switching the channels back and forth between a *Law & Order* rerun and a shoot-'em-up starring John Wayne, who seemed to be getting sexier as I aged. It was a boring, blustery Sunday night. We had been married for five years. I made room for Aaron on the couch; he came and sat down.

"She does?" I knew he occasionally spoke on the phone to his ex-girlfriend Lori, now married and a new mother. He'd never mentioned getting together before. I'd been curious to meet her.

"We can say no," he said, his usual response to social invitations.

"Say yes." I put my arm around him. He was wearing the light green shirt I'd bought him; he looked good in green.

"Why?"

"It'll be fun," I said.

"Real fun. The two of you can shrink each other all night." (Lori was a therapist.) He made his eyes bug out like Jack Nicholson in *The Shining*.

"Now that she's married with a kid, it's not threatening for her," I said, aware that her child made it threatening for me. I'd won

Aaron, but she'd won the fertility contest. I wanted to see her baby, out of morbid fascination.

According to Aaron, Lori was pretty, smart, shyer than me, and petite. More hovering, which I'd guessed was the tie-breaker. Her fatal mistake, during a slow work season for him, was to suggest he try advertising.

For two days I hounded him to make a date with Lori. He'd done it, he announced, for the next Saturday night. Eight o'clock. They'd come downtown. We'd go someplace casual. No need for a reservation. I was excited and bought a new black sweater for the occasion. More illuminating than meeting my own exes could be meeting one of Aaron's.

It was amazing how one phone call from the past could make a marriage more interesting. I feared I'd been flaunting my exes, like a matador's red cape, to get the attention of my husband. That week I peppered him with Lori questions. What was it like, dating a shrink? ("I don't know.") Wasn't it hard to stay friends after their breakup? ("I don't know.") How could he trade a tiny, soft-spoken, good listener for me?

"Every lover is a reaction against your last," he offered.

"I know I'm in trouble when *you're* quoting Erica Jong."

Friday night Aaron came home and said, "It's off with Lori."

"Why?" I'd never met any of his exes before. I was disappointed.

"She wanted to bring her baby." Aaron shook his head, like this was the craziest thing he'd ever heard.

"Maybe the sitter canceled."

"That's what she said. Come on. She's meeting my wife for the first time and there's no other baby-sitter in all of Manhattan? She's a shrink, for Christ's sake."

"I know, it's great. A baby between us, like a wall." I was intrigued with the possibilities. "Or it could be a weapon."

"I canceled. No dinner with babies!" he yelled.

Babies continued to be our sore spot. Though we were still trying naturally, after several gut-wrenching conversations, Aaron refused to talk more about operations, in-vitro, artificial insemination, or adoption. It wasn't fair. Denying your spouse children was a good reason for divorce. What would his defense be? "But judge, I can't stand it. My wife wants to have my baby!" I wasn't even allowed to see his old girlfriend's baby!

A few days later, he came home from work to announce that Michelle, another former lover of his, who'd become an actress, had showed up for a voice-over job on his animation show. He'd dated her for two years, twenty years ago. That was the problem with allowing in exes—everybody had a bunch they could pull out of a hat. Since the Lori liaison had fallen apart, he probably thought he owed me one. But hanging out in the past was getting pathetic. It was bad enough reliving getting dumped by *my* exes; I didn't need to be rejected by his. Was he being competitive, ready to unearth five of his old sex partners to spite me? I felt guilty about finding my exes and this was starting to seem like fair punishment.

I pictured a chorus line of his previous partners, all divorced and size three, holding up babies who needed fathers. An already-born infant would seduce him into fatherhood, in a way that I couldn't.

"I hope you're not thinking of hiring her," I told him. I'd been here once before, and lost. "George hired an actress for his play and wound up sleeping with her," I reminded him. "Don't hire her." George was the last man I'd loved before Aaron. The scenarios were similar. No such thing as an accident, right?

"Don't be ridiculous. I'm not sleeping with her," Aaron said. "Michelle is married."

"So are you!" I said. I vaguely recalled that Diana-the-actress-slut was engaged when she met George. "Is Michelle happily married?"

"Actually, she's separated," he answered. "She's beautiful. I'm sure she won't have trouble meeting a man. Men always loved her."

At the beginning I had liked it that Aaron was relentlessly honest. Yet after five years of marriage, his honesty had begun to seem lazy, like he couldn't make the effort to lie or at least monitor himself.

"She has two kids. She's going through a rough time." He dug himself in deeper.

I remembered when George first told me about his new actress, whom he'd cast as Ophelia or Kate the Shrew, I forgot which. "She's going through a rough time. She's so grateful I hired her," George had said. All men liked wounded birds. Now that I'd mended my own wings, I couldn't compete.

"You've described a beautiful, lonely, needy woman who wants to work with you every day from ten to midnight," I told Aaron. "You want to be the hero."

"You were actively digging up your exes, you hypocrite," Aaron said. "Getting together, having lunch. You're still e-mailing. Michelle was a total coincidence. She had no idea I was one of the producers of the show."

"How do you know Michelle didn't know?"

"Don't tell me how to live my life." Aaron's teeth were clenched. He turned on his computer, turning his back to me. "I hire who I want."

After our fight about Michelle the animation actress, he didn't kiss me good night. He was gone when I woke up in the morning.

When he didn't call by noon, I left a message at his office. He didn't return it. That was unlike him; he always returned my messages right away. As freelancers, there were enough important idiots who didn't return your calls. Marriage meant you had to. At 6 P.M., I e-mailed him. He ignored that too. Oh God, I'd defanged my exes but had refanged my husband!

Aaron was wrong about my continuing communication with the ex brigade. I no longer initiated contact, though three of them had recently sent me news. Richard had e-mailed to say that he and his wife, Beth, were getting divorced. Brad wrote that he and Kim (who was now twenty-five) were getting married. Then Tom let me know that he'd landed a new girlfriend and law job. Though in each case I tried to respond with the appropriate "mazel tov" or "I'm sorry," the truth was that all of my old boyfriends had lost their luster. They'd been demystified, reduced to friendship. That's what I'd been doing these last six months—I had successfully de-clawed my past. I hadn't counted on Aaron's past, which all of a sudden seemed more perilous. By midnight I'd worked myself into a frenzy. I pictured him taking Michelle out to a fancy dinner up-town to celebrate her starring role as Girl Alien.

"Sue's been hounding me to have a child," he'd complain. "She won't let up. She never listens."

"Pierre hounded me for more kids," Michelle would say as they clinked glasses. "He wouldn't listen when I said my baby-making days were through. In fact, I had my tubes tied."

"Really?" Aaron's eyes would light up. "Your tubes are tied?"

Locating my lost loves was a way to hide out in my history. It was simpler than facing the future with a husband who wouldn't be the father of my children. Yet the thought of losing him to some-one else jolted me. Women loved Aaron. After every business trip he'd mention some cupcake slipping her card into his pocket on the plane or sending over a drink at the hotel bar. I'd never worried before. But he'd had more girlfriends than I'd had boyfriends. If we divorced, it would be much easier for him to replace me. A fifty-year-old tall, successful male with great hair was a better prospect than a forty-year-old bitter, childless wreck. The world was unfair.

Yet not being able to get pregnant had left Aaron drained and humiliated too. Instead of soothing him, I made him feel inadequate. I was letting it destroy our marriage. No wonder he was turning to someone else for solace and sexual reaffirmation. I had done just that, five times. I'd sought old boyfriends to remember myself younger. In the process, I'd pushed away my husband.

When Aaron walked in at 2 A.M., he went into his den. I followed him.

"Sorry." He threw his keys on the desk. "Auditions went late."

"You didn't return my messages."

"I haven't been to my office all day," he said.

"Or my e-mails."

"I was at the studio twelve hours, I didn't check." He took scripts out of his briefcase. "We just finished. I'm zonked. I have to crash." He looked at me as if there was something he had to tell me but didn't want to.

They'd hired Michelle. He felt attracted to her. They did have dinner tonight, didn't they? Had he kissed her? "Aaron?" I stood up, walked toward him. His shoulders seemed bigger, as if he'd been secretly working out. He had never looked sexier than at that second, when I thought he'd leave me for someone else. "What is it? You can tell me."

"Nothing. We didn't hire her," he said. "We wound up cutting her part."

I went into the bedroom to change into my slinky black nightgown, along with Claire's maybe-they-were-Cinderella sandals. I sauntered back to my husband's den, turned off his computer and pulled him down to the floor of the Bat Cave, on top of me. I put my hands over my head and placed both of his palms over mine, as if he were pinning me there, locking me in. I squirmed and rubbed against him, trying to break free, pretending he was a big mean stranger, holding me down against my will.

"I know I don't say it enough, but I've never loved anyone as much as you," he said. "Every day I feel so lucky to have you."

"What, honey?" I shifted around, put his hands under the silk, and rocked back and forth to keep the rhythm going.

"You're so beautiful. Do you know how much I adore you? Sometimes I can't even remember what my life was like before you," he prattled on and on. I was losing my concentration.

"Shh," I finally said, putting my hand over his mouth. "Be quiet. You're not allowed to talk."

23

On Tuesday I woke up alone. Aaron was gone. I hadn't heard him get out of bed or shower. I vaguely recalled he'd mentioned a meeting uptown. Tuesday was such a dumb day for a fortieth birthday to fall on. I knew he was going to surprise me. He liked mysteries. I hated them, read the last page first to avoid the agony. If I was going to be disappointed, I wanted to get it over with.

There was no present in the bedroom, so I stalked the living room. No boxes, no balloons, no flowers. No new Dylan bootlegs on the music shelf. No new books. I went to the kitchen. No candy. No champagne chilling in the freezer or refrigerator. Not even a twelve-pack of my favorite, caffeine-free diet Coke, with a red ribbon around it, which worked like a charm on Valentine's Day. (Especially since it came with our version of him making dinner—take-out sushi he'd put on real plates.) There were no phone messages. I checked. Twice.

Well, who cared. Aaron, who did everything late, often argued that marriage came with a gift leeway: since nobody was going anywhere, nothing had to appear on the exact day. I had a present for myself anyway. I went to the bathroom—nothing in the hallway—and ripped open a nicotine patch. I stuck it on my back. The beige square, which looked like an oversized Band-Aid, itched. Change was good, I told myself. When in doubt, aim for health.

Tony, the doorman, buzzed to say I had a package. I ran down five flights of stairs to find forty roses. The card said "Happy Birthday Baby," and was signed "Love, Mom."

"Anything else come?" I asked him.

"No," Tony said. "Nothing."

I placed the lovely long-stemmed roses in a vase. The deadline was here. With my legs up on the couch, I waited for the agony to hit like an earthquake or incurable illness or at least a rainstorm I was caught in the middle of. For six months I'd been dreading this day. I was no longer a child. I no longer thought I could have one.

Lighting the lilac-scented candle on the coffee table, I stared into the flame, expecting the end of my baby dream to drown me with loss. But all I felt was relief. No more blood tests or standing in line at Duane Reade, hiding half a dozen cheap ovulation kits under my arm. No more four-hundred-dollar uptown appointments with specialists who ordered complicated, expensive, invasive, humiliating procedures. No more nightmares of babies with brain degeneration or arguments about insemination by a Russian cabdriver. No more fighting with Aaron.

I looked around our apartment, which seemed spacious and glamorous, the perfect size for a couple. My office in the corner, and the artwork on low shelves, could stay where it was. We'd made a warm, comfortable home here, in the city I'd chosen. I opened the black shades; it was sunny out. I was starving. I ordered in *The New York Times*, the *Post*, and a bagel from the corner deli.

"No cigarettes today?" asked Emad, the counter guy I was friends with.

"No. I quit. Don't ask me if I want cigarettes again!" I shouted at him.

"You want the white or yellow gum?"

"Three packs of both," I told him. "It's my birthday."

"Good luck," Emad said. "The gum is on the house."

When I hung up, I noticed Aaron's computer on my desk. Why had he put it there, pushing my black typewriter to the side? Confused, I walked to the Bat Cave and saw that Aaron's computer was on his desk. I realized the slender black laptop in the living room was mine. Aaron, that sneak, had left my present right in front of my nose.

I opened the lid and pressed the "on" button. It worked. I looked for my e-mail, typed in my code, and heard "Welcome, Profsue123." There was mail—thirty-seven messages! I no longer had to go through my husband's or father's or brother's account. Profsue123 had her own account; she was no longer a guest.

The first message was from my brother Eric, who wrote that he'd cleaned out my system folder, installed AOL, Microsoft Word, and the printer driver. I had no idea what that meant, but followed his instructions to download an attachment he'd sent. A picture of his precious little two-year-old Andrea, holding up a Barbie birthday card for Aunt Susie, unscrolled on my screen. It was in color, with music playing. Andrea was waving. Was it a video? How did he do that? I imagined Eric, my cyberdoc, before a row of computers in his Ann Arbor office, magically fixing mine.

When he'd nixed medical school to become a programmer, I worried that Eric would feel estranged from the other men in the family. Yet he promptly hooked up Dad with a state-of-the-art desktop. You needed a scientific language to communicate with my father and Eric had found a new one. He hooked up Brian, Michael, and now me. He'd been working on Mom, who was even more technophobic than I was.

"It's your fantasy," I e-mailed Eric. "Now nobody in the family will have to see each other in person."

"Happy birthday to my favorite sister," Brian wrote, adding that the software, already installed, was from him. "If Sammy and Dara could learn to use a computer before they turned three, you can learn at forty."

"Is that a vote of confidence?" I asked.

Though we were too close in age and eternally competitive, it made sense that Brian had became a trauma surgeon. He was loud and commanding. Growing up, I thought his machismo was belligerent. But he came through when you needed him. "If anything bad happens, he's the guy you'd want in charge of saving you," Monica once swooned. I had to agree, even considering the source, remembering the way he'd shown up to my (white) wedding the day his first child was born.

"You're only getting better," was the next message, from my youngest brother, Michael, in Chicago. He'd sent me a gift from an on-line used-book emporium specializing in first-edition poetry collections. Currently on its way to me were Yehuda Amichai's *Love Poems* and Pablo Neruda's *Twenty Love Poems and a Song of Despair*.

Nice double entendre with "getting better," I thought, especially from a heart doctor. Also interesting that a busy physician and assistant professor who avoided serious relationships was sending me love poetry. When he was born, my mother looked at him and, still under sedation, said, "He's a boy, Susie." Michael, who had my dark streak and insomniac tendencies, also wrote poems but had sworn me to secrecy.

I thanked him, saying a silent prayer that he'd soon find love too.

"Happy Birthday," said the note from DRKCAJ, Dr. and then Jack spelled backward. That my father had become a computer fiend in his late sixties still stunned me. He claimed to be looking up AMA postings and the on-line *Physicians' Desk Reference* till all hours. Mom was sure he was combing the Internet for porn. "His new mistress," she said. "At least I can unplug her."

"If your old man can learn how, anybody can," he wrote, signing it "DRDAD."

Then I found Aaron's message, which said only: "Taking you where no man ever has." I laughed out loud.

I'd never wanted a computer. I felt betrayed when Aaron abandoned his IBM Selectric and brought home an Apple laptop. He taught me how to use it for my NYU e-mail. He even came up with my screen name. There was already a Profsue, Profsue1, and Profsue12 out there, he'd checked.

I'd known for years that I should have taken the leap myself. I was a writer, for heaven's sake. I needed my own PowerBook; I liked the name. It took the males in my life to usher me into the new century, help me shoot my words into cyberspace. Why I couldn't buy one for myself, I'd analyze next week.

So on my big day, disaster did not strike. I sat at the new screen, touched by the conspiracy of my husband, father, and three brothers, five men who never broke my heart. (Just kicked it around a bit.) Stuck on what wasn't there, I'd almost missed what was. For everything important, I was late.

24

I can't believe I had to cancel Nobu for this dive," Claire said as we walked in.

"My birthday, my choice."

It was actually three nights after my birthday. I'd insisted she take me to dinner at the Chinese/Japanese joint down the street. I'd taken Brad here six months before, the perfect backdrop for a heartbreak interview. The restaurant was comfortably pathetic, the decor tacky, food mediocre. Nobody spoke English well so they screwed up the orders. A haven of low expectations. It had become a safety zone during my first hellish days of nicotine withdrawal: nonsmoking and they had big cheap bowls of edamame, green soybeans I chewed endlessly. (You sucked the little beans out, discarded the pods.)

It was empty for a Friday night, just a loud Asian family at a circular table in the middle. There were twelve of them—babies to grandmothers. I blocked bad memories of large family dinners as I led Claire to a table for four in the back, the farthest away. Seeing me, the waiter brought over edamame and a diet Coke.

"Make it two," said Claire. She'd also stopped smoking again three days ago, in sympathy. We'd been smoking since we were thir-

teen and quit together often, though it never got easier. She turned
to me. "You look pretty."

"You look gorgeous."

"Feel like death," she added.

"Me too."

Still, it was great having Claire in my neck of the woods. I'd
liked it best the year we both had studio apartments in the same
West Village building. We'd borrow money, clothes, cigarettes,
and joints every day. I'd never recovered from her move uptown.

She put a black Barneys bag on the table and I opened it. Inside
was a pair of high-heeled Prada fuck-me slingbacks, like the ones
I'd stolen from her and had just given back a week before. "Too expensive." I caressed them. We'd both been size nine since we were
nine; I knew they'd fit. But I liked hers better. Nothing like a well-
worn-in shoe.

"Or you can have mine and I'll keep these." She smiled. "But
you have to come uptown to switch them."

"Tomorrow." I petted the shoes. They were a nice metaphor.
Shoes were for moving. Sexy high ones, to walk taller. By now a
sushi maven, I ordered us a bunch of maki rolls, pieces of fish, and
more edamame. She draped the purple pashmina I'd bought her
across the chair. I'd given her warmth, color, and Gary, who she'd
been dating but never brought up. I wasn't allowed to ask.

"You're not supposed to eat soy if you want to get pregnant,"
I said, chomping on a bunch of beans. "But I'm not ovulating
anyway."

She gave me an annoyed look. Her cell phone rang. To my dis-
may she answered it.

While she talked to a client I recalled how my mother said she'd
never gotten over Claire's mother moving to Aspen. Not that thousands of miles was comparable to a cab ride from the Upper East
Side to the Village. Yet missing Claire felt familiar, love connected

to longing. I'd once started a poem: "At her party she thought only / of who wasn't there."

"Sorry," she mumbled when she got off.

"Tell me what's wrong."

"I'm sick of hearing how you can't have a baby," she said.

Where was that coming from? Maybe it was harder for her—being childless and husbandless. But it was my big birthday dinner—I deserved to wallow in my body's failure if I felt like it. I put the sandals back in their package and placed them on the chair next to me. "Why?" I finally asked.

"You're lying to yourself."

"No I'm not." I ate more beans, stacking the rinds in a separate plate. "I happen to be one of the most self-examined, honest people on the planet."

The waiter brought our rolls and sushi, with two pieces of flying fish roe I didn't order but it wasn't worth explaining. I went for the ginger, eating it all, self-conscious that he'd overheard her call me a liar.

A little Chinese girl who looked about three ran up to us.

"Hi honey," Claire told her.

I looked over at the table she'd escaped from, wondering why her parents let her run all over a restaurant. She stared up at Claire, then at me, seemingly fascinated. I gave her a tiny wave but was glad when her mother came to claim her. She carried her back to their group, where she belonged. Claire's eyes followed her.

"I'm so honest that some of my friends tell me I should start lying."

"When you really want something, you fight for it. That's what I admire about you." She picked up a shrimp with chopsticks and dipped it in my low-sodium soy sauce. "When you wanted to write for *The New York Times*, how many years of rejections did you ignore?"

I held a green pod between my lips and said, "Wonder if we can smoke them."

The waiter brought more ginger and extra wasabi. I ordered another edamame.

"Remember those rejection slip parties, where you taped your rejections on the walls?"

The memory embarrassed me. I'd done that in my twenties, when I assumed the rejections were temporary. "What's your point?"

"You've written for all of them. You literally wouldn't take no for an answer."

When had I switched from gifted child to symbol of perseverance?

"You did it with love too. You kept getting your heart broken, but you didn't give up," she said. "Then you hooked up with all the old ones. It was almost like you needed to have a rejection party with your exes."

"Wait a minute. That's facing down the truth. Where am I lying?"

"You try to have a baby for a year, then cry victim when you don't get pregnant."

"It's been almost three years," I said.

"Of trying naturally," she clarified.

"We spent ten thousand dollars on specialists, tests, and drugs that did nothing." I took the lemon out of my soda and put it on the napkin. I hated lemon.

"You freaked out at a few needles."

"I had blood work done *six* times!"

"You wouldn't give yourself the shots." She picked up my lemon and squeezed it into her soda.

"I have a lifelong fear of needles. I took fertility pills instead."

"Do you know what women who really want to have children go through?" she asked.

"I really want to have a child!"

"If it's convenient."

"You know that Aaron can't."

"I know that if you were sure you wanted to be a mother, you'd be inseminated by a donor or invitroed ten times by now. Or flying to an orphanage in Russia or China."

"You're wrong," I said.

"I would be too." She caught my eye.

Over the years, whenever I needed to figure out something important, Claire would tell me: "Let yourself know what you know." In that moment I knew neither of us would have children.

I flashed to a dinner with our families in Michigan when we were kids, all twelve of us at a pizza place where you threw peanut shells on the floor. Claire and I had been put in charge of the boys. When Teddy, her youngest brother, spilled his water, her mother made Claire clean it up. She tried but made a mess with the napkins. Claire's father reached over and angrily pinched her leg under the table. "That's not fair! It's Teddy's fault!" I'd screamed. My mother glared at me. There was no air-conditioning in that sweaty peanut room. The table was too small. We'd begged to be excused. Finally they let us. We'd run out to the parking lot, breathing in freedom and patting each other on the back, old war buddies at ten.

"Gary says to tell you happy birthday," she threw out casually.

"What's with you guys?" Though I hardly ever asked her, I'd made Aaron e-mail him to find out. "She's the greatest," Gary had answered. Hence we knew they were doomed.

"It's not working out," she said. "He's nice but I'm not that physically attracted to him."

"What's Dr. Z. say?"

"She thinks it's better to keep somebody around, like a science experiment," she said. "Can't we just blame everything on our mothers being pregnant four times together?"

I laughed, but it was an issue that had confused us for decades. "They got all the babies," she said. "There's none left."

"We gave ourselves things they couldn't."

"Manhattan. Work. Our own money," she listed.

"We just couldn't compete in their arena," I said. "Or we didn't want to."

"Both of their mothers died young," she said of the grandmothers we'd never met. "Women who lose their mothers young desperately need to be mothers."

"To become what's missing." I picked the avocado out of a piece of California roll and put it on her plate. She liked avocado.

"What was missing for us again?" she asked. We were like orphaned twins telling each other the story of our birth over and over. Each time it came out a little different, depending on what we were going through.

"Attention and respect," I told her.

"You're a journalist because at the end of family arguments you wanted to say, 'I'm right and here it is in the newspaper to prove it.'"

"Your brothers wouldn't let you play with their Lego and Tonka toys. Now you get to be in charge of all the buildings," I said.

"We chose careers over motherhood," she said. Or was she asking?

I nodded, rechewing the edamame pods, making a mess. "*Huge* careers. You're at a top international firm, I work for the best publications in the country."

"But after their kids went to college, our mothers worked. They got both."

"Barely," I said. "They only wished they could have careers like ours."

"You really believe that?"

"Sometimes," I said.

"My mother told me that after her mother died, she couldn't

get close to anyone. She admitted she couldn't even get close to her own kids."

"She said that to you?" I reached for her hand, but Claire pulled it away, fumbling for something in her purse. My mother was warmer than hers, more love had seeped in. It somehow seemed connected to why I could give myself a good husband.

"How did you know it would work with Aaron?" she asked.

"He didn't get what he needed either. So we have to take care of each other."

She took a piece of salmon. "That's sweet."

"How is our dual emotional damage sweet?" I took a piece of fake crab.

"You heal each other," she said.

The waiter brought two more bowls filled high with more green beans.

"We didn't order these," Claire told him.

"We give you free for ordering most edamame ever," he said.

Finding this hilarious, she roared. How could someone so sad have that round, deep, joyous laugh? I couldn't help but laugh too. The little Chinese girl, in her pretty red dress, ran up to us again, as if our laughter had summoned her. She danced around our table. Then she ran back.

"Next year at Nobu." Claire put down a gold credit card the waiter picked up.

"Is that like 'Next year in Jerusalem'?"

"Nobu's more expensive."

"I just needed a low-key birthday."

"You're such a control freak," she said.

"I am not."

"Who else would find five men who broke her heart to confirm she married the right guy?"

"Now that was a science experiment."

"I forgot what the conclusion was," she said.

"I saw the exact moment where I'd screwed up each relationship."

"I love that all the screwing up led to Aaron," she said. "He's the best guy who ever lived." When the waiter brought the bill, she signed it. "What did he get you for your birthday?"

"He went in with my dad and brothers on a laptop. They'd been planning it for months."

"I just got a shiver," she said.

"I know. I felt so loved."

"I was thinking the same thing when I saw my father last night."

"I didn't know your parents are in town." I felt a twinge; usually they invited me to dinner with them.

"My mom's at Canyon Ranch. I took Dad out to dinner."

"Just the two of you? How was it?"

"The most intense talk we've ever had," she said.

"What did he say? I can't believe you haven't told me yet. You buried the lead."

"He said he was proud of me. That I was the most successful career woman ever in our family."

"He said that?" I was amazed. "Talk about approval. Now that's a shiver."

"I know." She smiled shyly, then reached for her coat.

I saw the little girl watching us from her table but pretended I didn't. "See? It's never too late to have a happy childhood," I said as Claire and I walked out arm in arm.

25

I flew to Detroit Metro airport on Sunday afternoon for my annual summer visit. My father was waiting in his car, in front of the baggage claim. I got in and kissed him hello. Then I noticed a wooden cane in the backseat. He'd said, over the phone, that he'd fractured his hip. No operation was necessary, it would heal itself. He'd never mentioned the cane. A doctor who avoided doctors, hospitals, and medicine, he refused painkillers, just took aspirin. At home, it took him a long time to get out of the car. He usually carried my black bag inside, but I grabbed it and threw it over my shoulder.

It was hot and sunny outside. After kissing my mother hello and unpacking, I changed into my black bikini and went out to the backyard for a quick swim. I walked through the gate and down the wooden steps to my beloved pool. It wasn't in great shape. The white tiles were chipping. Branches on the oak and willow trees had grown longer, casting shadows, leaves littering the water. I draped my towel on a dusty lounge chair. I flicked through stations on the radio. My old favorite, 101 FM, had changed from classic rock to hip-hop since the last time I'd visited Michigan. My father usually took meticulous care of the pool. I put my toe in the water; it was freezing.

He opened the side door and yelled, "How's the water?"

"Too cold to swim," I said. "Is the heater broken?"

He nodded. "Sorry. I called the pool guys to fix it. They're coming first thing tomorrow," he said.

Monday morning I went out to wait for the pool guys to come. I really wanted to swim. I hated waiting, wanted a cigarette. Swimming would make me feel better. I hadn't smoked since my birthday, but I wasn't over the emotional withdrawal yet. It felt worse than a breakup. It was much easier to banish men from my life than cigarettes, though sex and smoking appeared connected.

"Come on, we put twenty penises in our mouths every day," Claire once said.

"I know." I'd agreed to the phallic theory. "All that sucking and feeling happy."

It was no coincidence that David, my first boyfriend, smoked. Yet my next lover, Brad, never allowed me to smoke in front of him and broke all my cigarettes. Some kind of castration? Freud said, "Sometimes a cigar is just a cigar," but he was a lifelong nicotine addict who'd died from it. I'd read that Freud's father was also a smoker. The summer George and I tried to quit together, George had said, "It's much harder for you. Your father smoked." That was another problem with quitting: intense memories surfaced from nowhere, a parade of ghosts I thought I was done with.

I looked up to see my father's silver Cadillac pull out of the driveway. He hadn't come down to check the pool's motor or whirlpool before he went to work, like he used to. Had I done something wrong? Then I realized it wasn't personal. It was too hard for him to walk down the wooden steps. I sprayed on sunscreen. The sky, bright when I'd looked out my window, turned darker. Everything seemed haggard: me, the pool, the house, my poor father—who, my mother said, was in constant pain but wouldn't admit it.

At eleven o'clock, the pool truck showed up. Two young Mexican guys tooled around the house, examining the controls and filter, fixing the heater, yelling at each other in Spanish.

"The water looks like it's getting lower," I told the short one. I used to be self-conscious in a bikini when the gardeners or pool guys were here. Now I no longer cared. "You should check that out."

"Yes, yes," the tall guy said, as if he understood perfectly.

"The water will be higher up tomorrow?" I asked. "And warmer?"

"Swim tomorrow," the other one said. "*Sí, Sí.*"

I brought them Coke and cookies, bribing them into fixing it faster.

Tuesday morning I rushed out and saw that the pool had no water in it.

"Mom, something's wrong with the pool," I opened the side door and screamed in.

She came out, looking upset. "I know." She pointed to the lawn next door, which was flooded. "The neighbors called. There's a big leak. I told your father it was stupid to keep using Pete's Pools after Pete died. He won't listen."

My father came out, walking with the cane, looking ashen and embarrassed, as if the pool was a patient he'd misdiagnosed. "I called them again," he said sullenly, trudging back in.

The men from Pete's Pools came back Wednesday. All afternoon they paced, worked, and fiddled with plaster and hoses while I sat on the lounge chair, reading and fuming at the weird empty tub I couldn't swim in.

"Much better," the short one finally said as they packed up to leave. "Swim tomorrow." I didn't offer them Coke and cookies this time.

On Thursday the pool had water in it, but it was brown and green. Sand lined the bottom. My father came out to survey the damage. He shook his head, defeated, as if he knew he was no longer a match for this huge monstrosity in his backyard. He looked exhausted, Ahab losing out to the whale. "I'll call them again," he muttered.

"We should try another company," I said. "Mom's hairdresser, Ricardo, has a great pool. His guys . . ."

"I'm not calling Ricardo's pool guys."

"Dad, your guys don't know what they're doing. They're like Cheech and Chong," I shouted. "They keep saying 'All fixed' and it gets worse."

"Who?" he asked.

"Those potheads in the movies. Never mind. Let me call someone."

"I'll get it fixed myself!" He turned to go inside.

I sat there for hours, sulking at my pool-less fate, enraged at myself for insulting my father. I hated to see him hurt. Instead of helping, I was making it worse. Finding old boyfriends I'd loved and lost was nothing compared to the fear that I could literally lose my father, the male I'd loved first and longest. Suddenly I worried that I had tracked down, interviewed, and reconciled with all of the wrong men. What if the only man I needed to remeet was him?

I thought of Claire's recent dinner date with her dad and tried to think of the last time I'd gone anywhere alone with my father. When I was three years old, he'd taken me to Candy Cone, bought me chocolate marshmallow ice cream, my favorite, with sprinkles. We were living in an apartment in Oak Park, ten minutes from his hospital. It was the last time he wasn't working a hundred hours a week. The ice cream parlor was around the corner. Did I remember his huge hand holding mine as we passed the swing sets, or was my recollection from a photograph?

When his car pulled up the driveway at five o'clock, he went right inside the house. I put on my coverup—the worn-out extra-large button-down shirt I'd taken from his closet a few summers before—and marched into his den. He was sitting at his computer. "Dad, remember when we lived in Oak Park and you used to take me to Candy Cone?"

He turned around and looked at me blankly. "What's Candy Cone?" he said.

I was stunned. How could he not remember? I ran up the stairs, surprised to find myself crying.

"What's wrong?" My mother came out of the kitchen, stopping me.

"He doesn't remember Candy Cone," I blurted between sobs.

"Are you having a midlife crisis again?" she asked.

"The same one; it's not finished," I laughed through my tears.

My father came out of his den, stood at the bottom of the stairway. "She's not smoking, makes her crazy," he offered.

"You would know, Cookie Monster," she said. He'd quit again too. Or rather, switched his addiction to oatmeal raisin cookies. "Every morning I find a trail of crumbs by the sink."

I took *The New York Times* up to my old pink room and spread the newspaper on my bed. My father came upstairs and stood in my doorway. I ignored him, reading the arts section.

"How long did you go to that school Roeper for?" he asked. "How many years?"

"I don't know." Why was he bringing up the school I'd attended from sixth to twelfth grade? I'd skipped eleventh, which made it six. "Six years."

"Who drove you to school every day?" he asked.

"You did!" I answered. He did! How could I have forgotten?

He'd offered to drive me on my first day, saying it was on his way to work. He had a blue Chevy then, which he always drove forty in the thirty-mile zone. The same redneck cop kept ticketing him. At least twice a month. He paid the tickets from his office. "Don't tell your mother," he used to say. I never did.

"Don't say I never took you anyplace," he added, triumphantly.

"Can I take you out to dinner tomorrow night?" I asked. "Just me and you."

"Why?" he said.

I looked at him.

"Ask your mother," he told me.

She said: "He's all yours."

I chose my favorite local diner for our Friday night date, The Village Place. Naturally, I liked the name. My father drove; he was driving slower these days. I chose a booth by the window. I ordered the chef salad, he got a hamburger.

"I'm sorry about the pool," he said. "I know how much you like to swim."

"It's not your fault."

"Cheech and Chong are idiots," he admitted. "It's like *The Old Man and the Sea.*"

"I was thinking Ahab."

"Good. The pool's the whale." He nodded. "Or 'Captain, My Captain,' " he said, reminding me that he was the first person who taught me poetry. "When's Aaron coming?"

"Sunday," I said, but I didn't want to talk about the broken pool or my husband. I'd waited decades to ask him something. I wanted to know what had gone wrong with us, why we'd never really been that close. I'd always thought it was connected to his complicated relationship with his sister. "My shrink once said I remind you of Shirley," I started.

She was his only sibling. They were close in age and looked alike. She'd died in her fifties. I'd always thought my father was haunted by not being able to save her.

"You and Shirley were so contentious," I said.

"No, we weren't," he said. I assumed his denial would be the end of the conversation, but he continued. "Not me. Shirley was always fighting with your grandfather. He wouldn't pay for her college because she was a girl. That destroyed her."

"Grandpa did?"

"Yeah. That's why, on the day you were born, your mother and I swore you'd get a good education. We'd go into debt if we had to."

"You swore that?" This I'd never heard before. "When I was born?"

"Yes." He nodded. "No matter what, we'd pay for any private school you wanted. I would have sent your brothers too, but they hated Roeper because it didn't have a gym."

I'd always thought he'd favored the males in the family. Yet my father had actually paid more for my education than for theirs. And they took the bus, he never drove them.

When the waitress came with our order, he took a big bite from his hamburger. I picked at my salad. His food looked better. "I was lucky Roeper was on your way." I stole a slice of pickle from his plate.

"Well, I switched hospitals. So after the first year it wasn't," he said.

I was amazed. "Why didn't you tell me?"

"I'm telling you now." He sipped his soda. "What else do you want to know?"

"You're sure I don't remind you of Shirley?" I asked. She couldn't have children either.

"Shirley had a tragic life," he said.

"I'm not tragic," I told him.

"No, you're not," he agreed.

Was that why I wasn't tragic? Because when I was born, before I even knew it, he'd saved me?

"I thought, since Mom was light-haired and sweeter . . ."

"Your mother's tough. She's not so sweet," he said.

Uh-oh. Was something wrong with my parents? "Are you guys fighting?"

"No. What time does Aaron's plane get here on Sunday?"

"Four o'clock."

My father sloshed ketchup on his fries and ate a bunch with his fingers. "He's a good man."

I took some fries too and dipped them in his ketchup. I should have ordered fries. "I know."

"We were very happy when you married him."

"Me too."

"I was so afraid that you'd never get married . . ."

"Okay," I cut him off. "Quit while you're ahead."

When we finished eating, I could tell he was antsy, he wanted to go. I grabbed the thirteen-dollar check and insisted on paying. I'd bought my father books and presents over the years. Aaron had taken my parents out to dinner, but I'd never picked up the check.

"I'm leaving the tip," he said, throwing out two singles. When he stood up, he stopped, wincing.

"Are you in pain?"

"Getting better," he nodded.

I touched his hand. "Are you sure?"

"Your mother doesn't like weak men."

"What?" I stared into his eyes. He was still handsome, just grayer and a little more tired.

"Nothing."

"Don't be silly. She adores you. She drives thirty miles to get the exact oatmeal raisin cookies you like . . ." I stood up and hugged him.

He hugged me back and stroked my hair. I would have liked to hold him longer, but he let go.

"Let's get out of here," he said.

At home, he went into his den. I went upstairs to my bedroom. Sitting on my pink bedspread, I called Aaron in New York. No answer. I tried his cell phone, like he'd instructed me to when I couldn't find him at home or his office. He didn't answer that either.

"Why did you get a cell phone for me to call you if you never pick up?" I said into his machine and hung up. Then I went online to e-mail him. Before it connected, the phone rang.

"Hi," he said.

"Hi," I said. "I just called you."

"I know. I don't know how to work it yet."

"I was about to e-mail."

"If you fax too we'll have a media blitz."

"You just don't want to be reachable."

"I'm more reachable to you than I am to myself," he said.

"Dad wants to pick you up at the airport Sunday. I hope you're not checking luggage."

"I have to."

"Why?"

" 'Cause I'm carrying on the Shapiros' greatest food hits. Zabar's blintzes for your dad, Second Avenue Deli chopped liver for Brian, Carnegie Deli's chocolate bobka for Eric, and Gus's pickles for your mother. I'm glad Mike's in Chicago, 'cause adding his Mongolian barbecue would have killed me."

"You're not gonna schlep pickles on the plane again?"

"Two pounds of sour dills," he said. "Why? You don't like your man smelling like Gus's pickle juice?"

"As if they don't like you enough," I laughed.

"Now you'll never get rid of me," he said.

I went into my parents' bedroom. My mother was sitting on the king-size bed, watching the news on TV. She was wearing a lace nightgown, tucked under the green silk comforter. I sat down next to her. She scratched my back with her long nails, like she used to.

"How was your shrink session with your father?" she asked.

"Will you be nice to him?" I said.

"He sits in his den, on that stupid computer," she answered. "Barely even talks to me."

"He says you don't like weak men."

"He said that?" She smirked slyly, as though this was some ancient secret between them. "We're fine. What kind of lies is he telling you?"

"Was Dad contentious with Shirley?" I still hadn't quite ironed out the intergenerational family link.

"Always. Like cats and dogs," she told me. "But it was worse with your grandfather. He was always bothering Shirley."

"About what?"

"Her clothes, her hair. Her dates. He was so controlling and intrusive, he made Shirley crazy. That's why she married Ira Katzenberg so young, to get out of her father's house. Your father once said he never wanted to bother you like that. He didn't want to chase you away."

What I thought was benign neglect all these years was really him being respectful? No wonder I was always getting my signals crossed. Or was he? "I thought I reminded him too much of Shirley."

"You remind him too much of him. You're clones. Reclusive, pig-headed, nicotine-addicted workaholics. With those ratty old shirts you won't throw away. Everyone on his side of the family is self-destructive," she said. "Oh, his pool guys came again. They replaced the filter and fixed the heater. It should be better tomorrow."

"Let us pray."

"Did you break off the branches from the trees outside?" she asked.

"Yeah, they get in the way of the sun."

"What's wrong with you?" She stopped scratching. "Don't break off the trees."

"Is the backyard for the trees or the people?" I asked.

"You're the only idiot who still sunbathes." She shook her head.

"That's what Aaron says." He hated sitting in the sun, burned quickly, like she did. "He's bringing you a present."

"I would die for a Gus's sour dill," she said.

As I walked to my room, I realized I hadn't emulated my mother, I'd married her.

The next morning I went to the pool. It was filled to the top, like normal. I put my toe in. The water was frigid and mucky, leaves and dead bugs floating to the surface. Some fixed filter. Damn it all to hell. I threw off my coverup and jumped in anyway, forcing myself to swim two laps in the slimy cold, crawling fast, thinking I'd get used to it. But I didn't. I was about to climb out when I saw my father, standing by the fence. His face lit up when he saw me in the pool. So I stayed in, hoping to please him, forgive him, get over him already. Shivering, I thought of the Stevie Smith poem about the woman in the ocean, "further out than you thought," who was either waving or drowning.

"All fixed?" he called out to me.

"All fixed," I waved.

Acknowledgments

I would like to express my deepest gratitude to . . .

My fantastic, amazingly perceptive, inspiring editor, Danielle Perez, who said "Yes!"

My brilliant, understated agent, Elizabeth Kaplan, who e-mailed "this one's not bad."

My Midwest pal Laura Berman, who said, "You have no imagination whatsoever. Write a memoir."

My steadfast Tuesday night writing workshop for saying, "You should have gotten old and bitter a long time ago, 'cause this rocks!"

The late, great Howard and Bette Fast, who said, "Be nice to her. She's meshpocheh."

My patient, encouraging colleagues Roberta Bernstein, Alice Phillips, Sandy Frazier, Kathryn Stern, Sally Arteseros, Melanie Fleishman, Ruth Gruber, Gary Kordan, Nicole Bokat, Lance Contrucci, Devan Sipher, Marilyn Berkman, Gerry Jonas, Vicki Polon, Karen Salmansohn, Wendy Shanker, Jill Hamburg-Coplan, Amy Koppelman, Matthew Flamm, and Judy Burdick, for reading millions of pages.

My guardian angels Carolyn Hughes, SG and Molly, for their loyalty, love, and laughter.

My editors over the years (especially Harvey Shapiro, Ed Faine, Julie Just, Michael Anderson, Michael Molyneux, Frank Flaherty, Faye Penn, Irene Copeland, Susan Korones, Emma Segal, Suzy Hansen, Maria Russo, Dwight Garner, Peter Bloch, Mark Cunningham, Sara Berman, Rona Cherry, Carole Braden, John Strausbaugh, Sherry Amatenstein, Lynne Schreiber, Joy Press, Penelope Green, Eric Copage, Stan Mieses, Yona Zeldis McDonough, and Esther Haynes) who said "The check is in the mail"—when it really was.

My L.A. liaisons Gary Rubin, John Ufland, and Jody Podolsky, who said, "I can see Helen Hunt in the lead."

My N.Y. dream team, Karin and Dan Brownstein, Shannon Jamieson, and the hysterically funny Barb Burg, who responded to my first straitlaced author photo by saying, "What's with the books and blazer? You look like a college professor."

Patty Gross, who said, "Everything you ever thought about love and marriage is wrong."

Fred Woolverton, who said, "Don't trust any instinct, you're always wrong."

My warm, wonderful parents, who said, "Go ahead, tell the whole world you're in therapy."

My kind, extremely supportive brothers, Brian, Michael, and Eric the computer doc, who said, "I can merge your Microsoft files, fix the formatting, and e-mail your book in half an hour."

My fantasy in-laws LuLu and Isaac, who said, "You're the best thing that ever happened to him."

My beloved husband CR, who said, "Just make Aaron's penis bigger."